PRAISE FOR *The Jeweled Highway*

"Written with a poet's eye and a seeker's urgency, Ralph White traces his spiritual journey. His hunger for truth leads him down many alleyways. He rewards the reader with hard-won wisdom."
— JULIA CAMERON, author of *The Artist's Way*

"A riveting, deeply joyful spiritual adventure demonstrating how a sustained wish for truth can attract a life strewn with inner meaning."
— JACOB NEEDLEMAN, author of *An Unknown World: Notes on the Meaning of the Earth*

"As a leading figure at the New York Open Center for three decades, Ralph White has introduced thousands of speakers, none more interesting than himself. In this gorgeously written memoir, the evocative images of his wide and deep life journey inspire us to do likewise — seek and find, again and again."
— ROBERT MCDERMOTT, president emeritus, California Institute of Integral Studies, author of *Steiner and Kindred Spirits*

"Ralph White is talented, original, and uninterested in convention, and his life has been an adventure of the Joseph Campbell kind — a quest to find the secrets of life and then give them to his fellow citizens. He is one of those rare men who has said yes to life far more than he has retreated into safety."
— THOMAS MOORE, author of *Care of the Soul*

"This *Jeweled Highway* of Ralph's is really cool. I greatly enjoyed traveling on it through his vivid account of the challenging adventures, and the internal discoveries they spurred, which resulted in the no-nonsense, good-humored, and spiritually activated person he is today. He has served all of us — who insist against all odds upon a better world — so creatively as the sophisticated spiritual impresario of the historic, catalytic New York Open Center, a place where so many have opened their minds and hearts to see deeper and dream greater. In this highly readable memoir, he colorfully describes his ups and downs and brave wanderings through far-off landscapes of the earth and of the mind and spirit. If you're one who wants to know where we've been and where we're headed in these times of great danger and opportunity, I cannot recommend it highly enough."
— ROBERT THURMAN, Professor of Indo-Tibetan Buddhist Studies, Columbia University, author of *Inner Revolution* and *Infinite Life*

"What an extraordinary memoir. Ranks among the best books I've read in years! What a privilege to be so intimately invited into the inner life and breathtaking adventures of such a great seeker and person of action as Ralph White. He is a living 'Center of Consciousness' for the whole world."
— ROBERT SARDELLO, co-director, The School of Spiritual Psychology, author of *Silence: The Mystery of Wholeness*

"What splendid adventures-in-life await within this book! What a true jewel that avoids all dogma and instead seduces us with outrageous explorations of the soul. What a timely literary miracle in this era of spirit-questing and esoteric regeneration."
— DAVID YEADON, author of *The Way of the Wanderer: Discover Your True Self Through Travel*

"This is a brilliantly written autobiography of self-discovery from one of the foremost cultural creatives of our time. Like a contemporary Odysseus, Ralph White invites us to join him on his spiritual journey and absorb along with him the distilled wisdom of the human race that he encounters along the way."
— KYRIACOS MARKIDES, author of *The Mountain of Silence* and *Inner River*

"*The Jeweled Highway* is a rare beast, a compelling book of spiritual vision and inspiration that is also an exciting adventure story — a 'ripping great yarn' — and a testament to human courage and the willingness to push into the farthest frontiers in search of wisdom and spirit. In offering this memoir of a life very well lived, Ralph White also takes us on the most important quest of our time: the journey into the heart and soul — and magic — of a world in transformation. I enthusiastically recommend it!"
— DAVID SPANGLER, author of *Journey Into Fire* and *Apprenticed to Spirit*

"*The Jeweled Highway* is not about one man's personal quest into the mysteries of the unknown. It is about the innate human longing for the existential truth that originated with the first prehistoric utterance, was amplified through cavernous netherlands, and was embodied for centuries in forbidden books and secret societies the world over."
— ALNOOR LADHA, executive director of The Rules and board member for Greenpeace International, USA

"Like a skilled caravan driver, Ralph White leads us into the heart of the esoteric Western traditions — a luminous landscape forgotten by the spiritual tourists of Eastern wisdom ways — and reveals the jewels hidden there. His own inner and outer adventures uniquely qualify him as our insightful and big-hearted guide."
— MIRABAI STARR, translator of John of the Cross and Teresa of Avila, author of *God of Love: A Guide to the Heart of Judaism, Christianity and Islam*

"Ralph beautifully and vividly chronicles his journey of a meaningful life. For anyone on this path, his recollections are both inspirational and motivational as he helps the reader understand that life's meaning can be searched for both through mystical experiences of intuitive guidance and through conscious, thoughtful choices. I am often asked about the history of the human-potential movement, and Ralph has adeptly captured the nuggets of what was taking place in the '60s and early '70s. It is a unique read — a story captured through the eyes of one of the successful founders of the holistic-center movement."
— CHERYL FRAENZL, director of programs, Esalen Institute

RALPH WHITE

The Jeweled Highway

ON THE QUEST FOR A LIFE OF MEANING

For Rober,

In Brotherhood

Ralph White

7/18/19

NY open Center

DIVINE
ARTS

Published by DIVINE ARTS
DivineArtsMedia.com

An imprint of Michael Wiese Productions
12400 Ventura Blvd. #1111
Studio City, CA 91604
(818) 379-8799, (818) 986-3408 (FAX)

Cover design: Johnny Ink
Editor: Ross Plotkin
Printed by McNaughton & Gunn, Inc., Saline, Michigan

Text set in 11-point Plantin with headings in 28-point Filosofia

Manufactured in the United States of America

"We Gotta Get Out of This Place," words and music by Barry Mann and Cynthia Weil.
Copyright © 1965 by Screen Gems–Columbia Music Incorporated, USA.
"Route 66," words and music by Bobby Troup. Copyright © 1946 and assigned to Londontown
Music.
"Give Me Love (Give Me Peace on Earth)," words and music by George Harrison. Copyright
© 1973 by the Material World Charitable Foundation Ltd.
"Guinnevere," words and music by David Crosby. Copyright © 1973 by Stay Straight Music.
"Hello Muddah, Hello Fadduh," words and music by Allan Sherman and Lou Busch. Copy-
right © 1963 (renewed) by WB Music Corp. and Burning Bush Music.

Chapter Nine: A Request from the Oracle of Tibet was originally published in a somewhat
different version entitled "A Walk on the Wild Side" in 2003 in a Travelers' Tales edition entitled *Tibet: True Stories.*

Library of Congress Cataloging-in-Publication Data

White, Ralph, 1949-
The jeweled highway : on the quest for a life of meaning / by Ralph White.
    pages cm
  ISBN 978-1-61125-034-3
1. White, Ralph, 1949- 2. Spiritual biography. 3. Pilgrims and pilgrimages. I. Title.
  BL73.W46A3 2015
  204'.4--dc23
                              2015002121

Printed on Recycled Stock

CONTENTS

PART ONE: *The Quest*

PART TWO: *The Work*

PART THREE: *On the Jeweled Highway*

For Nanette

For all my family in Britain and Ireland

And for Clare and Janna

ACKNOWLEDGMENTS

This book would not have been completed without the invaluable support and dedication of Nanette Schorr. I am deeply grateful for her creativity, editorial taste, and unswerving focus. Nor might the book have emerged without the encouragement and enthusiasm of Michael and Geraldine Wiese of Divine Arts — a heartfelt thank you to both of them. I also want to express my appreciation to Judith Pintar for reading the manuscript and offering extremely insightful suggestions on structure and content. My thanks go out to Thomas Moore for graciously contributing the preface and doing so simply from the goodness of his heart. Others who read the book before the final edit and gave me honest and helpful suggestions include Linda Kirk, Nancy Maloy, and Seth Lennon Weiner. I would also like to acknowledge Ross Plotkin, whose meticulous editing made this a smoother read.

I happily offer deep thanks to Clare and Janna Fleming for contributing essential soul nourishment during the years of writing and beyond, and for holding a very special place in my life. The research on family history by my cousin in Cardiff, Shirley Newberry, has been of enduring value. This is not a book about relationships, but I must express my deep gratitude to my many friends and colleagues, and to the wonderful women who have profoundly enriched my life. The serene atmosphere of Cortes Island in British Columbia, where this book began to take shape, provided a silent and beautiful environment in which to begin the telling of this story. Finally, a shout out to all the speakers, writers, artists, philosophers, activists, and pioneers in and out of this book whose work enabled me both to develop a holistic worldview and find multiple opportunities to express it in ways that make a difference.

Preface

by Thomas Moore

One of the most terrorizing travel memories I have is driving a rental truck loaded with my wife's paintings to the New York Open Center on Spring Street for an extended show. To this Detroiter, Manhattan is as exotic as it gets, and I've had nightmares about driving a truck there. But what really astonished me was that a center of spiritual learning would care to exhibit sophisticated paintings by an artist in tune with the latest currents in serious painting. Clearly, something unusual was going on at New York's signature center of all things holistic — some openness of mind, some genuine taste, some inspired worldliness. That something was Ralph White.

To be honest, until I read this luminous memoir, I didn't know who Ralph White really was. I've always liked Ralph, with his Welsh blend of urbanity and pub-like grittiness. I know the Irish and I can see the influence of Ralph's mother in his intelligence, earthiness, and humor, but it is all tempered by his native reserve and thoughtfulness. His Welsh background to me means talented, original, and uninterested in convention.

At the Open Center, Ralph has encouraged me to make public any intellectual and spiritual impulse that possesses me, and he attends my seminars and takes me to lunch, where we have memorable conversations, and he is always planning yet another adventure back into history and forward into relevancy. Ralph is one of those rare men who has said yes to life far more than he has retreated into safety. In both external and internal realms, he is an adventurer, a blend of Indiana Jones and Herman Hesse.

His life would have to be portrayed by a youthful Harrison Ford, but Ralph is also Carl Jung and Ralph Waldo Emerson. In these exciting tales of a life really lived, you may be surprised to discover that such a bold adventurer ends up in a spiritual center of holistic programs in the heart of Manhattan. I think you have to understand the subtext of his autobiography: He is most interested in the *cauda pavonis*, the peacock's tail that is the endpoint of alchemy, than in any fame for having conquered an actual mountain or wasteland. His life has been an adventure of the Joseph Campbell kind — a quest to find the secrets of life and then give them to his fellow citizens.

For me, the ultimate value of this beautiful piece of autobiographical writing is to grant prestige and value to the late twentieth century and early twenty-first century search for spiritual insight and well-being. I don't think you'll doubt the gravitas of spiritual types after you read Ralph's account of his coming into awareness. You'll see how a man could be steeped in the culture of his time and yet intelligently transcend the paltry values of his situation in a genuine quest for spiritual integrity.

In the story behind the story, we see Ralph's gradual discovery of a life vision and purpose as he follows the signs and opportunities, traveling from one part of the globe to another. He has many true adventures that are revealed to be the school that prepares him for his work as an impresario of spiritual matters. But all along, his route takes him through gritty scenes of humanity rarely at its finest. Ralph's way makes him compassionate but not too sweet, appreciative of traditions yet not stuck on any one.

The glaring weakness in modern spiritual movements is a dismal failure in thought. Generally, spiritual practice is in, while theological thinking is out. Ralph rebounded against the logical positivism of his university experiences, but who today would know enough about that philosophical detour to shun it? Ralph is not an intellectual, exactly, but a thinker. He can see value in the human-potential and spiritual movements he lived through. He perceives their philosophical challenge to the modernist, materialistic ways of the modern establishment, and he has a philosophy of his own, focused on beauty and transcendence and vitality and fed by a love of history and tradition that allows him to raise spiritual movements to a high level of significance. He may realize, more than the presenters of his courses, the fundamental challenge of a visionary way to the death-driven path of modern politics and culture. As you read Ralph's memoirs, you can't help sensing his awareness of history and the retrieval of traditional rites and ideas. The Open Center has a Zen emptiness at its core and a welcome for all serious thinkers and players at transcendence.

Academics and intellectuals may not fully appreciate the kind of university Ralph has created in various forms throughout his life. They are not aware of a simple dictum from Freud: Intellectualizing is a form of defense. I believe that they are reacting against, protecting themselves from, the vitality of Ralph's brand of vision. If nothing else, this book is vital and alive and not constrained by ideology or political correctness. It is Dionysian, a voyage without a plan, a trust in serendipity, an appreciation of love over logic. Ralph is willing to enter the grit of low culture while being borne into heights of neo-Platonic beauty. He can sway to the angel voices of Sufi mysticism and appreciate the cultural critique of the Beatles.

I see this book having the impact of Ram Dass' *Be Here Now*. It offers a rationale for idealism rooted in grit. He advocates being alive in the present while knowing your history, allowing your emotional and communal highs while realizing the gifts of insanity and the cultural fringe. Ralph's memoirs embrace the spiritual sphere of multiple revelations and portray a love of Gaia, our planet, as perhaps no one has done before. If some modern revelation has appeared on our planet, Ralph has been there, not in control, but willing to participate and be affected.

Here is where Ralph White's narrative offers direction to current voyagers and travelers on the way out of materialistic insanity into meaning. Don't glorify any truth or tradition. Participate. Participate. Feel the insights and discoveries of others. Don't restrict yourself to any truth. Open your heart to the most lowly practitioners of wisdom. Don't succumb to the lures of the sweet and the lofty. Remain loyal to the lowly and the grimy. Stay grounded, even as you explore the highest.

Trust your calling. Stay on track. Always use your own compass. Make extravagant decisions in favor of adventure. Always employ the principle of love. Keep in mind your deepest connections and loyalties: your family, your old loves, your homelands. Be an intellectual, but never fear the worthy opposite of anti-intellectualism. Be emotional and follow your feelings. Above all, create an absurd organization and live an unpredictable and serendipitous life. Don't expect logic and reason and sanity. Break the boundaries. Build a spiritual life in the most secular setting imaginable. Be outrageous. Trust your guidance. Teach, but don't inculcate. Enlighten, but don't convert.

This is Ralph White. His story is a guideline. You can trust it. It's your model. Do it in your own way. Travel outwardly, inwardly, or both. Look and be transformed. Follow your own daimonic guidance and don't give your soul away to anyone. Don't follow the money. Instead, follow the trail of spiritual transcendence offered you. Make your own New York Open Center wherever you are. Take your life seriously and let it be sculpted by your destiny, not by any practicalities. And never believe those who say that what you envision as a life's work can't be done. Whatever, whoever guides you can work miracles.

INTRODUCTION

A cold gray sea lashes the rocks on the west of Enlli Island. The sun is setting, blood red between fierce, high clouds. The swell pours its surging rhythm against the Island of the West, isle of 20,000 saints, at the far tip of Wales, land of my birth. The seagulls cry in their mysterious, plaintive way as they surf and swoop through the air currents. What is it that I hear behind those mournful cries that seem everywhere on the Welsh shore of the Irish Sea? Something is pulling me back, touching some kind of ancestral memory. They seem to hint at the lost holy wisdom of the Celtic island saints. The cry of the birds, the crash of the seas, the smell of the salty air, the feeling of distance from the hard and petty affairs of the world, and that pervasive sense of poignant mystery that clings to the rocky edges of western Britain and Ireland.

Freed of the mundane constraints of daily life, open to contemplating the eternal, moved by the vast and empty skies, my mind gazes rapt on the setting sun slipping into the crashing seas. Here in this psychically distant world, meta-thoughts of human destiny rise up from the mental places where they lie dormant in the rush and stress of city life. In moments like this, I can easily embrace the spiritual philosophers, the seers of the evolution of consciousness, and contemplate the spiritual future of humanity. This is the Tibet of the West, with its sense of being beyond the beyond, close to the transcendent, where the soul fills with the pulse of nature, the knot in the solar plexus quietly unravels, and the heart lifts up toward the empty sky.

For centuries Celtic monks on Iona in the Hebrides, Lindisfarne in Northumbria, and Caher off the coast of Mayo must have known this damp and windswept but exhilarating life — misery in the lashing rain, ecstasy in the luminous spring sunshine, the bleating lambs, the mainland mountains, the peeking buds of life returning. Always seeking the divine beyond the gray curtain of clouds, that eternal, steady, life-giving presence, the holy disk of the Sun, once known to the Irish as the god Lug, later understood by monks as the symbol of the Archangel Michael.

As for me, when I gazed on Enlli Island from the western headland of the Llŷn Peninsula, I knew an intense tingle up the spine, the feeling of the crown of my head lifting, the sense of sheer vitality springing up from the limestone and moss below my feet. Pure, cotton-white clouds softened the peaks of Snowdonia and the mountaintops of Central Wales, stretching south as far as the eye could see. The comforting sound of Welsh warmed my New Yorker's heart, that tongue from an ancient time far older than English, yet somehow still loved and used a mere day's journey from London. To be an aficionado of the Celtic holy islands is to be blessed.

A decade later, in the depths of urban stress, my memory returns to a serene and sun-filled evening gazing out to sea from Dùn I, a flattened hilltop on the isle of Iona. Silence fills the air, the harvested fields are turning golden in the late-afternoon light, the water is turquoise and smooth as glass. Fullness enters my being — calm, content. Somewhere a tractor's engine growls in the distance, a dog barks, a fishing boat comes into view. But I am suffused with tranquility, and a quiet joy seems to invade every cell.

Moments like this give us strength for a lifetime. They are inner resources, precious gifts, to be drawn upon when needed. In quiet meditation, how many times have I recalled that holy Hebridean serenity? More times than I can count!

I count myself lucky to have been born in the Celtic world, the son of a Welsh father and Northern Irish mother, spending most of my childhood on the Welsh shores of the Irish Sea, playing on the Great and Little Ormes, those limestone massifs jutting dramatically toward Ireland and the Isle of Man. I spent many hours as a child absorbed in the tidal pools along the rocky beaches, looking for small pearls in mussels, gazing at the sea, absorbed by the sight of darting, tiny fish amidst the seaweed and pebbles.

The "central myth of Western civilization," to quote Joseph Campbell, came from this part of the world. From these ancient islands, up from the deep heart of the Celtic imagination, come the tales of Arthur and the Grail and the Quest. What murmurs in the soul prompt the search for the elusive and mysterious chalice? What longing still stirs for some deeper stream of reality beyond the gray, dreary world of so much contemporary life, with its shopping malls and work for faceless corporations?

★ ★ ★ ★ ★

This book is the story of a quest for a life of meaning — emerging from the darkness of alienation. As an adolescent in the industrial north of England, I could see little purpose to human existence. The shadow of two world wars still hung over the culture. The legacy of the Industrial Revolution clung everywhere in my home-town in the thick, black soot that covered the surface of every building. Two hundred years of hard grind and subsistence for the world's oldest working class; centuries of small lives, poor diet, and grim labor conditions had left a pall of depression hanging over the place. Or so it seemed to me.

I had never adjusted well to the departure from Wales at the age of nine when the soothing Irish Sea and the distant mountains of Snowdonia were replaced by mills and factories, grit and grime. Within weeks of arriving in Huddersfield, I found myself walking to school in the morning in smog so thick that no homes were visible on either side of the street.

No doubt others loved the town and its people in the '50s. I have since come to appreciate them myself. But as a youth, I felt trapped, bored, miserable. And as I grew older and began to question the purpose of human existence, little was available as consolation. Grow up, get a job, get married, have children, retire, and die. That seemed to be about it. When I repeatedly asked what we were here for, people looked perplexed, as if the question itself was nonsensical. Yorkshire was all about brass tacks and practical matters. Forget that bloody stuff, lad, and get back to work.

But I couldn't. As a teenager, I watched a riveting television series on the Great War filled with exhausted, haunted-looking men in flat tin helmets staring wanly from the trenches amid the mud and desolation. This looked like the real world to me. What did the pious phrases of religious men have to do with the mass suffering and death that the world had known for half a century?

Not much, as far as I could tell. I found consolation in the great music emerging with outrageous vigor from the north of England. That sexual pulse, those soulful melodies, rhythm of life, vitality, and youth, all spoke to me with more meaning than anything I found in school. This was raw exuberance lifting itself out of the bombsites and universal grayness of postwar Britain to shout about love and sex and fun deep into the night. It was balm to my teenage soul. The lines from the Animals echoed around my head: "We've got to get out of this place / If it's the last thing we ever do / We've got to get out of this place / Girl, there's a better life for me and you."

But still the constant questions nagged at me in quiet hours. Alone at night in the front room by the dying embers of the coal fire I pondered the meaning of it all. How could any kind of divine being permit the horrors that the twentieth century had brought, from the Nazi concentration camps to the Stalinist show trials, from the trenches of Flanders to Hiroshima?

When I left home around my eighteenth birthday, new life was breaking out all over. The Beatles had grown moustaches, beards, and outrageously long hair, and psychedelia was on everyone's lips. But at university, the old philosophical clichés still reigned.

It was only when I came to America in 1970 that things began to shake loose in the compartments of my mind. Those endless deserts in New Mexico and Arizona with their grandeur, silence, and mystical beauty somehow awoke a remembrance in me of a state of consciousness behind and beyond my everyday awareness. Their vastness evoked a larger mind that I realized I had carried with me all my life but been mostly unaware of. Somehow, I could hear intimations of a deeper reality, a wisdom-filled cosmic silence that lay beyond my chattering, mundane thinking in the way that the stars lay beyond the prosaic rush of everyday life.

This was the moment I had, unknowingly, waited for all my life. Suddenly the shelves of bookstores were filled with volumes I had never noticed that spoke exactly to my new experiences. I realized that there was a powerful tradition here of Eastern philosophy, Western esotericism, and native shamanism that was entirely outside the acceptable canon of Western education. The star-filled nights of the Southwestern deserts had elevated my soul, and the day produced an altered state of consciousness as I gazed on the cacti, the canyons, the mesas and buttes that had been the background to countless Western movies of my childhood. I felt as though I was moving through a landscape of dreams.

After that first trip out West, nothing was ever the same. Doors opened in my psyche that I didn't even know existed. I had discovered a path through life that was about living, authentic spirituality, love, oneness, and meaning, and was as far removed from my dark musings in the bitter, grime-covered streets of my adolescence as I could imagine.

My journey since has required me to listen to that quiet but persistent voice deep in the heart's core. It has led me on quests into many new realms. Most of all, it showed me a way to contribute to the great awakening so needed by the world as it faces innumerable crises, both inner and outer.

I have been fortunate to find a path to an independent spirituality and to help create centers, vehicles for cultural change that serve as focal points for a new awareness now rising to meet the need for a sustainable future where soul and well-being return to their rightful place. This book's chronicle of a search for meaning is the story of a life devoted to awakening the beauty that lies somewhere at the center of every human heart. The tale may be unique in its details, but it is a universal story of spirit lost and found, of the work of cultural and spiritual regeneration now calling strongly to millions, and of the esoteric mysteries at the center of many cultures. My hope is that it will entertain and inspire those who, like me, set out on a seemingly hopeless quest for a deeper view of life and, much to their own amazement, actually find it.

PART ONE

THE QUEST

∞

CHAPTER ONE

THE BEGINNING OF THE STORY

WALES

M y Welsh grandfather, who died when I was five, had been a sergeant major in the trenches of the First World War. He had been temporarily blinded by mustard gas, and his eardrums had been burst by the cacophony of artillery fire at the Battle of the Somme. Somehow, he appears to have survived four long years in the mud and misery of Flanders, and was awarded the Military Medal for bravery.

Thomas Herbert White had left school at little more than twelve to work as a cleaner on the railways to support his widowed mother. Cardiff in those days was the world's busiest coal port, with trains bringing that black, dirty, chunky carbon down from the Rhondda Valley where it was loaded onto ships and sent worldwide in the days when coal was the primary fuel of the world economy. He was an intelligent man but he had been deprived of a decent education by the limitations of government policy, and by the poverty of his widowed mother, who had been left alone after her husband, an engine driver on British Railways, had died in his early forties following an accident in the driver's cabin.

We have a few family pictures of him looking smart, trim, and focused in his army uniform. His eyes do not betray the nightmare he must have endured in the trenches. Like my father, he seems to have been a dignified and honorable man. After the war, he could only find work as a welder and tester of ships' chains in Cardiff docks. The family narrative has it that he would walk miles to work each day, his lunch a few slices of white bread and margarine, work a twelve-hour shift, then return the same distance home on foot. He would often spend his lunch breaks chatting with a "tramp" who lived among the docks and whom he had come to admire for his unconventional life wisdom. His name was Ralph and, at my grandfather's suggestion, it became mine too.

My father volunteered for the army when war broke out in 1939. As a thirteen-year-old, he had passed his examinations with flying colors and had clear academic potential. But the family's poor circumstances meant there was no money for books, uniforms, and the other requirements of a decent grammar-school education. He had been lucky in Depression-era Cardiff to find a job as a telegram delivery boy working for the post office. He had even managed to save enough money for a motorbike. As a teenager, cruising the countryside with his pals was one of his greatest joys. It's hard to think of my father, a very correct and reserved man, as one of the early bikers. But that's what he was.

At the advent of war, he and his friends knew that if they volunteered to be army dispatch riders and brought their motorbikes with them into the military, there was a good chance they could both stay together and do what they loved best: travel through rough country at high speeds. I can only imagine my grandfather's mix of pride and sorrow at seeing his son put on the uniform in such dire circumstances.

In 1940, the 53rd Welsh Division was sent for training to Northern Ireland. On his first weekend of leave in Belfast, my shy father and his friend Viv were walking down the street of this unknown city when they spied two girls dressed in their Sunday best. My father would have been far too mortified to address these strangers in such a bold way. But Viv called out, "Hello, girls," and the young women, curious about these smartly uniformed soldiers, stopped.

Thus were sown the seeds of my incarnation. My mother, Myrtle, was working in a tobacco factory in Belfast, stuffing the dried leaf into packets and weighing them, and not unhappy with her life. The two Irish girls and the two Welsh soldiers talked briefly as they strolled together, and my mother-to-be somewhat reluctantly agreed to meet my father again when he had his next leave. As my mother tells it decades later, it was more a case of curiosity and the positive impression made by those crisp, smart uniforms than anything else that led to this first date.

Their marriage in 1941, within a year of the sudden, devastating deaths through illness of my father's sister and mother back in Cardiff, must have provided him with a new measure of emotional stability. But he never spoke about it much. "Don't worry about me," could be the White family motto, as my father was clearly guided by his own father's instinct to minimize gratuitous attention to the self. This was not a family in which one drew much attention to one's own suffering, or asked for much for oneself.

My mother had grown up in a big, loving Belfast family ten years younger than the next child. Gran Brown, her adopted mother, had been widowed in her mid-thirties with nine children. Her husband had gone to his brother's funeral on a cold day and had contracted pneumonia and died within weeks. Gran Brown took in this extra child for the sum of a hundred pounds and used the money to buy some cabins in County Tyrone that she could let out during the summers.

I've often wondered how she could possibly have survived in the 1920s with all those children and no financial support. But she appears to have been an enterprising woman who would buy fruits and vegetables in the country and then sell them fresh or made into jam from the front of her house on the Crumlin Road. In any event, no one seems to have starved. By the time my mother's first memories arise, her oldest brothers were already working as bricklayers, surveyors, and other tradesmen, and her sisters were smart, even glamorous young women who loved to go dancing on the Isle of Man to the sound of the big bands.

For my mother, it seems overall to have been a happy childhood. She had been welcomed into this big, rambunctious family in working-class Belfast, and always felt loved. When war broke out and Belfast was attacked as a major shipbuilding port, a cluster of incendiary bombs fell on my mother's street. Showing her innately feisty spirit, she and a brother, who were alone in the family house, were the first on the block to run outside and grab household brooms to put out the blazing, smoking incendiaries littering the terraced street. Inside that short five-foot body, there was a big heart with a lot of warmth and courage.

My parents married in 1941, my father still recovering from the loss of his younger sister Winnie to tuberculosis, and the death of his mother, Ginny, through a sudden stroke at the age of fifty a few years later. My mother knew little of Wales and its people. The wedding ceremony was brief; the best man's speech amounted to little more than "Let's have a drink." The wedding night was spent on a ferryboat from Larne to Stranraer in Scotland, the ship blacked out to avoid German U-boats.

In such a way, my mother arrived in Cardiff as an innocent twenty-one-year-old to live with her new father-in-law, and her sister-in-law, Olive, not knowing a soul in this country, surrounded by the stress and danger of war. She never seems to have thought of this as a courageous act, but to me it has always seemed very brave.

After a few weeks staying with my grandfather, my mother moved to the home of Auntie Olive Newberry, one of the great comedians and humorists of the family, whose house on Topaz Street in Roath was an endless round of laughs, comical moments, good humor, and social warmth despite the wizened presence of blind Auntie Annie in her green visor and pinafore.

She soon found herself caught in air raids in a strange city in a new country with a family she barely knew while her husband was stationed at distant army barracks. But she had found humor and warmth and welcome in the extended Welsh family, and we were to enjoy a reasonably happy home life in the initial aftermath of war despite the narrow streets of tiny terraced homes on Cyfarthfa Street in Roath where we lived.

Fun and always ready for a laugh, permeated by Irish sociability, my mother charmed most of the people she met in later life. As she aged, her most appealing qualities emerged most strongly, and people in America constantly told me how marvelous she was when she visited New York. Barely five feet tall, she was gifted with a social intelligence that I learned a lot from as I got older. Some judgmental teacher at school in Belfast had convinced her that she was stupid and she retained that feeling all her life. But she was far from stupid. She may not have had a huge logical mind, but she thought of ways to touch people's hearts. She never visited anyone without bringing a thoughtful gift. You could put her on a bus, and within a few hours, she knew everyone on it.

In wartime Wales, she found humor and welcome with her new family. My father stole away from army bases, often riding far across the darkened land on his motorbike to visit her despite the bombing raids and the corrugated-iron hut in the back garden that provided the only shelter. It was a time of danger and privation, endured with the nourishment and mutual support of a caring and close family. Despite the air-raid sirens, the bombs, and the inevitable fears, the family remained intact and flourished.

Like most British men of his age, my father endured and survived the privations and horrors of the Second World War. As an army dispatch rider he carried coded messages on motorbikes and jeeps from headquarters to the front, from the beaches of Normandy across northern France, through the liberation of Holland and on until the surrender of Germany. Unlike most, he had been required to stay in the army an extra year after 1945, initially to be trained to be parachuted onto the Japanese mainland in an assault wave, later to be sent to what was then Palestine to keep the peace.

His last week in the army he was in charge of guarding a radar station on Mount Carmel. The sentries had fallen asleep at their posts and allowed members of the Jewish underground to burst through the gates spraying machine-gun fire everywhere. But no one was hurt. To initiate a court martial would have required another six months after seven long years in uniform, and he decided to let the matter rest. Getting home to his wife and child in Cardiff, where he could start a new life in the post office, was his priority.

When it was all over, my sister Lesley and I experienced the world of austerity Britain. There were still years ahead of rationing, with mandatory spoonsful of concentrated orange juice and cod liver oil at Albany Road infants' school to enhance our modest diet. My memories of early childhood in Cardiff are filled with the laughter of family gatherings on Topaz Street, my cousin Roslyn and I always up to one trick or another, running and laughing on the terraced streets, making up crazy and dirty-sounding words, giggling at the washing lines of underwear put out to dry on the clothesline.

At the other side of town in Canton, my Auntie Olive Bonas, my father's sister, was married to Uncle Cecil, a train driver. Evenings spent there with my cousin Alan would be filled with the sounds of steam locomotives, the chug of engines, the smell of smoke, the sense of lives and people traveling away into the unknown, to mysterious destinations in a bigger world too vast for me to understand.

In 1953, when I was four years old, my father received a promotion in the civil service he had joined after the army and we set off to live on the coast of North Wales in the holiday town of Llandudno on the shores of the Irish Sea. After the working-class row houses in Roath, Cardiff — tiny terraces with outside toilets — the beauty of North Wales was stunning. We lived for a short while in a rented apartment near the foot of the Great Orme, and I walked to Lloyd Street Primary School, an old dark stone building in Llandudno next to the town's lifeboat. All the time the cries of seagulls filled the air, the limestone massif rose above us, the mountains of Snowdonia sat serenely in the distance, the salt spray tinged the air. The skies were big, the sea a heaving and mysterious mass, and the people friendly. It was a happy time. Men still touched their caps when a woman passed on the street, something hard to imagine fifty years later. Old sea mines from the Second World War still occasionally blew up on contact. The lifeboat next to the school was no ornament; it was a highly functional and consistently necessary source of rescue that had to launch at a moment's notice.

Everywhere there were little teahouses serving sandwiches and scones. The old Victorian pier jutted out into the Irish Sea with its loud and brassy amusements, its smell of fish and chips and candy floss, the stern cliffs of the Great Orme always present looming over us, huge, forbidding, exciting. At the top of the Orme, at the end of the cable car, was Randy's Bar, named for

Randolph Turpin, who had beaten the American boxing legend Rocky Marciano to take the world title.

Mostly this was a peaceful time, and a warm sense of neighbors and community pervaded Merivale Road, our newly built semidetached home not far from the seafront. After two decades of depression and war, my parents' generation was ready to have fun. Many evenings, my mother in her long, shiny dresses, my father in his best suit and tie, would go out to dinner dances at hotels in nearby Rhos-on-Sea. Festivity and laughter were in the air. If you had been forced through poverty to leave school at thirteen, then endured seven years in the army going from the second wave in Normandy to the German surrender, you were ready to enjoy yourself.

As for my sister Lesley and me, when the summer weather was beautiful we rode the open-air tram to school in the morning as it glided through the fields next to the Irish Sea, the sunlight glinting on the waves, the patchwork fields that make this part of Wales so charming glowing with light in the fresh sea air, the twin Ormes looming, the distant mountains emerging from clouds. I heard the rhythmic sounds of the Welsh language around me on buses and trams, in shops, in queues, and, increasingly, in school. Welsh came very easily to me though my father knew just the words and phrases he had learned in Cardiff as a schoolboy. Learning it was not an abstract task as Latin and French were later to be. It was a living language of warmth and community, and somehow I absorbed it without strain with the friendly help of Mr. Morris the Welsh teacher at Lloyd Street Primary School. When news came that we were to move to an industrial town in the north of England, I remember feeling a deep sense of regret that I would not finish learning Welsh.

It was hard to imagine what Huddersfield would look like. In those days before motorways when most people did not even have cars, the north of England was a distant world. All I knew was that we had to move for my father's job and that we would have to leave behind the promenade along Penrhyn Bay, our friends, the warmth and intimacy of a small seaside town, and the chance to clamber over the Ormes and wander for hours among the rocky tidal pools along the beach. Somehow, my young soul had absorbed the surging, constant rhythm of the sea, with its open horizons and feeling of limitless space. How I loved its beauty when, slate gray, it was tossed by storms, the creamy spume flecking over the sea walls, the relentless waves pounding the concrete barrier between sea and land, the nine-year-old boy gazing in wonder at the raw power of nature.

But a chapter of my life was coming to an end. It was the most idyllic time I had known. In my memory now, the only stains on this idyll were the occasional encounter with a schoolyard bully eager to take advantage of my sensitive nature, and my confusion on how to deal with it. What remains is a picture of a charmed world — innocent, friendly, small-scale, courteous. I knew then what it was to walk in beauty, as the Native Americans say, as each day I was surrounded by vast, open skies; the twitter of birds in trees and hedgerows as we crossed the Little Orme on the way to school; the slow-moving, white paddle steamers docking at the end of Llandudno Pier and sailing north to the Isle of Man in the summer months, their huge side paddles thrashing and churning, their old-fashioned red funnels smoking, and their hint of distant lands as they gradually disappeared over the horizon. Many years later, the coast of Wales still has the power to move me to the depth of my being.

A very different world was waiting for our family in the industrial north. As we left the sea-and-mountain landscape of Wales, our first encounter was the burning gas flares at a power plant south of the Wirral Peninsula, then mile after mile after mile of working-class terraced houses, traffic lights, grimy buildings, and glimpses of mills and factories. Warrington, Salford, Eccles, Manchester, Oldham — an endless procession of flat, shut-in, narrow streets. A feeling of depression and constriction gripped my heart and it seemed this dreary, poor world would go on forever. But then came the beginning of the moors and the road began to rise, the cities gave way to the lights of hillside villages, and we entered the bleak, inhospitable Pennines, their brownish grass and desolate farmhouses opening up before us.

CHAPTER TWO

∽∾

MILLS, DARKNESS, AND RAIN

By the time we reached Huddersfield, it was dark and we made our way to our new rented home high on Bank End Lane overlooking the town. I felt lost and worried. My father, uncharacteristically, had forgotten the keys, and we stood outside in the gathering gloom, frustrated and alone. Then my sister recalled seeing a film in which a thief had slid a newspaper under the door, pushed the door key from outside until it fell out onto the paper, then extracted the paper and gained entrance. It worked in the film and it worked for us. We were so grateful to have a home in this alien, harsh, dark place.

I awoke the following morning in 1958, and my heart sank as I gazed down on the mass of chimneys belching smoke into the morning air. All around me were the terraced houses of the working people who had provided the labor for the Industrial Revolution that had begun its global trajectory not far from this spot.

Somewhere in my soul, I must have resolved to leave at the earliest opportunity. For years after I gazed at airplanes, fantasizing that one might land near Huddersfield and give me a chance to step aboard and fly away from this dreary world. Would I ever get out? Would I ever escape the blackened, depressed world of pubs, Friday night fights, and dead-end jobs?

Years of tedious book learning at junior and grammar (high) school offered the only route to freedom. I spent countless bus journeys making my way back home from school, the rain lashing the bus as it swept down from the Pennine Mountains and ground slowly past the blackened woolen mills, the windows steamed up so that only vague shapes of factories and soot-covered buildings appeared in the fading light. At each stop tired working men in cloth caps climbed aboard and sat down behind me, telling each other of their struggles to survive and the small holidays they had taken in Blackpool or Scarborough, Northern seaside resorts on the English coasts, where beer, bingo, and cheap thrills seemed to offer the only break from the grind that had worn down their forefathers in the same exhausting, woolen mill jobs for the previous hundred and fifty years.

A curtain of depression descended on me. Would I ever get out? Was I doomed to live in this grim, industrial town forever? Far from the seashore and mountains of North Wales, I gazed each morning on the myriad factory chimneys and the rising plumes of smoke. I heard the flat cadences of the Yorkshire accent and I longed for the music of the Welsh voices, the sea over the next hilltop, escape from the dreary round of school and homework.

As a teenager, I was gripped by the work of Wilfred Owen and Siegfried Sassoon, whose poetry of the horrors of war in the trenches of the Somme had left me with an overwhelming sense of the futility and meaninglessness of life. I could see suffering and stupidity everywhere around me — violence, death, accidents, misery on the evening news every day. My adolescent philosophy saw little or no meaning in life. The only reason to keep on going seemed to be the prospect of another adventure or the possibility of meeting a girl — a rush of adrenaline or a surge of sexual excitement to keep the overwhelming sense of futility and aimlessness at bay.

Since late childhood, I had wanted to know what we were all doing here on earth. What was the point of existence? The notion of eternity haunted me throughout my childhood. I would lie awake at night thinking what it meant to live forever and ever and ever. Even if we had been good and made it to heaven, the thought of doing anything like playing a harp on a cloud forever and ever seemed like a nightmare to me.

Gazing out over the wide, empty moorlands day after day at school, finding my only serious scientific interest in the constantly changing cloud formations of this Northern big-sky country, I would wonder: How many years would it be before I could find freedom from this dreary, exam-ridden existence? I was restless and itching to experience a larger reality.

There were few occasions for exhilaration in those anxious teenage years, but those that existed were intense. My early forays into the world of hitchhiking provided many of the biggest rushes. One brisk morning, standing aged sixteen at the side of the Manchester Road, my thumb stuck out, watching the traffic grind past the mills and factories, suddenly it happened! A large commercial van pulled over and the driver beckoned for my friend and me to get in. As I ran towards the vehicle, a surge of ecstasy tingled up my spine and a thrilling sense of freedom seemed to enliven every cell in my body. Yeah! I might have no money, but I could hitch wherever I wanted. From now on, adventure was always available, and a first glimpse of freedom was granted, never to be forgotten. In those days there were many truck drivers who had been in the armed forces and had hitchhiked themselves across Europe during their national service or war years. They were often willing to give a couple of young lads a ride, especially on grim and wet days, and farmers would allow us to sleep in their barns among the hay and the mice while the rain pattered outside on the fields.

My sister Lesley was five years older than I was, and we experienced a largely harmonious relationship throughout most of our childhood. She was bright, sensitive, and practical, and she loved to read and learn. For both of us, the move five years later to industrial Northern England was a trauma and shock that took years to heal and integrate. Fortunately, while still a teenager she met an attractive Frenchman, Jean-Claude, one of the few Europeans in Huddersfield in the early 1960s, and married him a few years later when he had completed his compulsory military service as an officer in the French air force. This was just as well, as tensions at home had become difficult to bear. Adolescence was an explosive time in the family dynamic, only enhanced by a generation gap that was at its widest as the old postwar cultural order began to crack.

But on a clear day, Huddersfield was big-sky country like Montana. The moorland foothills stretched to the long, jagged ridge of the Pennine Hills, out on the horizon etched starkly against the Western sky. A constant wind blew down from Scapegoat Hill sending small white clouds scudding across the blue expanse. For a moment, I would feel free.

One winter day after racing cross-country on the icy ridges of Colne Valley, I stood in the school changing room after a shower. Someone had a tiny transistor radio hanging from a hook. A sound caught my ear and hooked me. Poignant, rhythmic, mysterious, the harmonica stopped me in my tracks and I strained to catch each note and phrase. "Love, love me do, you know I love you." There was something I'd never heard before: insistent, compelling, strange. I was riveted from the first few bars.

I was totally drawn to the Beatles, with their hair, their cool, their honesty, their total lack of respect for the class system that was still suffocating Britain. They were their own people.

The Beatles were heroes to me and to my classmates. Forget chess and birdwatching and bridge. I remember seeing a picture of George Harrison with a moustache for the first time. Facial hair on a pop star? Totally unknown in that clean-cut age. But it was the beginning of the unkempt, shamanic look, and as soon as I saw it I knew it was the look for me. Thank life for the saving grace of those years: rock and roll. Here was vitality, sexuality, rhythm, joy, a way to get out of my dark ponderings. And so the door began to open for me as a teenager to a life of freedom.

Still, my adolescent mind was gripped by the classic British television series of the 1960s on the Great War and the stressed, pale, frightened faces of young men about to go over the top of their trenches to the probability of death by shellfire, machine gun, or mud. I read books on the Nazi concentration camps and thought how impossible it was that some kind of benevolent, omnipotent God could have permitted such horror and injustice. What was this life really all about? Could it have meaning? Could there be some higher force invisible to the senses?

My classmates and I continued to endure endless examinations — the Eleven Plus, Ordinary Levels, Advanced Levels, Special Papers — most of it memorization of facts that have long disappeared from our memories. One thing I did know was that academic achievement was the only route I could see out of a dead-end world. Here, with a bit of luck, was my ticket to freedom.

I read an article about the new British universities. The one that caught my eye was Sussex, outside Brighton on the south coast of England. The first of the new universities established in the '60s, it was intended to break the stranglehold of Oxford and Cambridge on talented students, and its curriculum was imaginative and fresh. But mostly what attracted me was that at Sussex, an atmosphere of "hectic heterosexuality" was said to prevail. That phrase was enough for me.

When I went down to Brighton for an interview in the autumn of 1966, I was seventeen years old and felt like a nervous, anxious naïf from the industrial North surrounded by confident public-school boys and seemingly poised girls. After the interview, I noticed that in the common room of the School of English and American Studies, there was a loud, colorful mural with three prominent messages: TURN ON, TUNE IN, DROP OUT. At the time, I was too innocent to grasp the reference to Timothy Leary. But I did know that I liked the feeling of newness at Sussex, I was entranced by the girls in miniskirts, and a sense of impending liberation from the sooty and repressed town of my youth was rising up.

THE CLOUD BEGINS TO LIFT

My door to freedom opened in 1966 when I acquired the exam results I needed to get into Sussex, and was finally able to look with ease at the school system I was about to leave. A few days after my eighteenth birthday I left home to spend three months in provincial southwest France in the small town of Villeneuve-sur-Lot, halfway between Bordeaux and Toulouse, working in the garage and welding shop of my brother-in-law's family. Few people spoke English, and I was introduced to raw, rural French life with hours spent changing wheels and brake linings, sweeping the workspace, gazing with a mixture of desire and intimidation at the French women who haunted my adolescent imagination. The work may have been uninspiring but the sunshine, the lush fields of fruit, the liqueurs and *pastises,* the cycle races and go-cart competitions, and the immersion in unadulterated French culture and cuisine were fun and different after dark, gritty Yorkshire. I felt that I was beginning to live.

When I arrived at Sussex as an undergraduate in September 1967, I felt like I had walked into an enchanted realm. Maybe not everyone felt that, but a lad from Huddersfield certainly did. The grassy campus seemed both sophisticated and relaxed.

Would I measure up in this new world of academic excellence, an experience no one in my family had undergone? The overall feeling of this time in my life is one of light, expansion, freedom, and entry into a world of intellectual inquiry. There were brilliant professors — Leslie Fiedler was visiting from America after being thrown out of his professorship for smoking a joint. Zevedei Barbu, an encyclopedic sociologist in exile from Romania, gave awe-inspiring overviews of the history of social thought. Marcus Cunliffe in American Studies and David Daiches in English poetry were among the most knowledgeable academics in Britain in their fields, and the former was an accessible, open man.

The academic I felt closest to was my personal tutor, David Morse, whose knowledge of American literature, and irreverent and intelligent take on social and academic issues on both sides of the Atlantic, resonated well with me. Sussex was trying to break the mold, to inject new life into the stuffy world of British academia dominated for centuries by the Oxbridge old-school tie. And it succeeded, at least for me. The university was a true opening to a bigger life. Academia was not the path I chose in my life, but Sussex was an essential step to freedom. The relief was huge!

Sussex was thought to be the academic counterpart of Swinging London in the late '60. September 1967 was indeed the literal high point of the miniskirt, and beautiful young women were shaking off the shackles of sexual inhibition. A major challenge for me was the difficulty of reading in the university library when young women in micro-miniskirts would saunter by with their tantalizing flashes. Life was now intellectually stimulating and culturally freeing, and erotic intensity was everywhere for me.

After years of schoolteachers in their imposing gowns refer-ring to us humble students imperiously by our surnames or, if we were very lucky, as gentlemen, I met my first university teacher. I walked up the tower to her office, a little anxious about the intel-lectual firepower I was to encounter. I knocked. A female voice rang out, "Come in." I entered and found an attractive, youthful blond woman with booted and mini-skirted legs upon her desk and an open, welcoming American smile smoking a thin cigar. I had clearly come to the right place.

Yet despite the rising protests about the war in Vietnam, the fabulous rock and roll and early British-blues boom, and the sense of a culture in deep change, I was not fulfilled. All my life I had waited to study philosophy and to grapple with the deepest questions of the human condition. Neither school nor clergy seemed to offer me answers to deeper questions. Now I hoped that philosophy would do the trick. But we were offered A. J. Ayer's *Language, Truth, and Logic* as our opening book, and my heart sank as I attempted to find sense and meaning in these tautly argued but emotionally empty paragraphs. One evening as I stood in line at the refectory, I heard another student tell a friend how he had thrown his copy of this book against the wall in pure frustration. To this day, this still seems to me the most intelligent response to the philosophical dead-end known as logical positivism. To find these ivory-tower dons reducing the most profound questions of human existence to wordplay and semantic analysis, caught in clever twists of logic that led nowhere . . . this was deeply disturbing. I had finally found my way to the hall of the philosophers, and it looked like nobody was at home.

Ah, well, thank God for rock and roll. Sussex was fortunate to have Jimi Hendrix and the Crazy World of Arthur Brown at the student union, and Brighton offered Fleetwood Mac at the King & Queen pub, Cream at the Dome, Traffic at Jimmy's Blues Club,

Pink Floyd at the Pavilion, and a host of lesser-known bands who made the early years of smoking dope a musical revelation. My student friends and I would wake in the morning after a trip to Jimmy's, the electric hum of the outrageously loud music from the night before still ringing in our ears, the soulful licks of the blues guitar still speaking eloquently of the emptiness and hurt of modern life. Here was a depth and passion that no contemporary philosophy was approaching. Here was the transmuted suffering of the Mississippi Delta reborn in modern British life, where spiritual poverty had replaced the material poverty of the sharecroppers and cotton pickers.

I came to love Sussex and Brighton, their great music and air of accepted sensuality and the new vistas opened up by the university courses. The first lecture I attended at Sussex was on "Revolution and Psychedelia" by David Cooper, a colleague of R. D. Laing. The psychedelic era was all around, with Gandalf's Garden, *Sgt. Pepper*, and "Set the Controls for the Heart of the Sun." Would the halls of academe ever meet the psychedelic cowboys of rock and roll? I had little inkling of it at the time, but I realize now that my life required me to engage with this question.

As for my girlfriend of the time, Jenny, all I can say is that she was beautiful, highly erotic, and loved rock and roll and short skirts. She introduced me to the realm of extended sexual and romantic pleasure, and I will always be grateful. When I met her at a party in 1969, the burdens of my life began to slip away. I recall her intense mascara, Dusty Springfield style, accentuating green, expectant eyes, wide and teasing; her clear and uninhibited delight in the erotic; her willingness to pursue me when I was still so closed down and emotionally unavailable that I couldn't even say yes when life offered me a gorgeous helping of delight.

My early experiences in '60s Brighton were a revelation to me. I began to see how closed down I had become, how my own self-protective shell was putting a barrier between me and the world. One very bright, clear, sunny day, I was walking down the Brighton seafront when I suddenly noticed the beauty of the contrast between my shadow on the sidewalk and the sun-covered paving stones. I'd never noticed that before. How minor an observation, but how major a shift! I was suddenly becoming aware of the beauty of the world around me after sustained enclosure in a gray shell of my own making.

Watching a stick of incense as the smoke formed perfect spirals, a piece of fresh apple mixed with Cadbury's chocolate in my mouth, my stoned friends giggling in the background, I began to realize how good life could be, how much wonder there was in the simplest of things around us. The play of sunlight on the English Channel, the ornate Victorian form of Brighton Pier lending dignity to the pebbled beach. "Lovely to see you again, my friend. Walk along with me till the next bend."

Things were looking up. Jenny had brought with her the ecstatic realm of the erotic; music was expanding my mind; and I was about to finish my degree. Suddenly it seemed that I was finding references to mystical experience everywhere. Was this what the American Transcendentalists were talking about? It was obviously what the Beatles and many others were writing and singing about.

It was all young and unformed, but the seeds of a new world-view were emerging. Everything I experienced was contrary to the dull positivism of the philosophical establishment with its hopelessly dry rationalism and its disinclination to engage with the deeper questions of the meaning of existence.

By 1968, America was lurching out of control. Assassinations, riots, war, and a deep feeling of contempt and hatred were brewing between the hippy, counterculture protesters and the redneck, military culture of violence. I had chosen to focus on American Studies. To study America was to engage with the most engrossing phenomenon of the day. In my leisurely late-1960s mode, I learned a fair amount about the United States from Marcus Cunliffe, Leslie Fiedler, and others, but it was time to go and discover what the fuss was all about.

I decided to apply for a place in graduate school in America. After all, I had been studying the culture for three years, and wanted to experience it firsthand. I knew nobody on the continent, so I applied for graduate school through the English-Speaking Union, a stuffy and privileged bastion of the establishment based in Berkeley Square in Mayfair, the most elegant part of London. When I went for my interview, I was the only non-public schoolboy there. I peered nervously around the hushed, thickly carpeted waiting room at the pinstriped, well-cut suits of the other candidates. I overheard the Oxbridge accents, the sense of unassailable self-confidence of these sons of privilege with their short, trimmed hair, and felt that I had no chance. My hair was long; my goatee was clearly alternative; I did not own a suit; and my voice let any class-conscious Englishman quickly know my non-U Northern background.

Fortunately, there was a professor from Sussex on the interview committee, and he was kind. He asked me about Eldridge Cleaver and *Soul on Ice*. My answer must have sufficed, and I learned a few weeks later that I had been accepted to apply to graduate school through the English-Speaking Union.

That last summer in England took on a sweet and poignant glow. Jenny and I lived in Hove, the stuffy but often elegant town adjoining the west of Brighton. I taught Scandinavian students — mostly beautiful, blond teenage girls — the rudiments of the English language and British culture. It was 1970, and all they wanted to do was go up to London, see Carnaby Street and the Kings Road, and taste that moment of rebellion, freedom, and music when the whole world's eyes were on Swinging London. I gave them freedom and independence, and they were grateful.

The memory of that last ride to Stansted Airport to catch my flight to America remains with me strongly. My father, ever the well-prepared dispatch rider, had the route worked out as we headed into the woods of East Anglia. The sky darkened, rain began to fall in torrents, and we could barely make out the airport with its post–Second World War Nissen huts and air of remoteness. But it was only after I passed through customs and stood on the far side of a glass barrier that the emotion of it all hit me. Jenny and my parents were only an inch away behind the glass screen but they were already a world away. I had been blasé, on top of the situation, ready to deal with it on the long ride down. But now it was here and my heart was wrenched.

I did not know it, but my life was about to change irrevocably. My love, my family, my security, my intimacy, my support were about to disappear as I boarded a plane for the first time in my life amidst the rain and darkness. Was I prepared emotionally? Would I be able to handle this strange, demanding world on the other side of the Atlantic?

I had booked a cheap flight on the unfortunately named Saturn Airways, a charter outfit that ran flights of drafted soldiers to Vietnam and ferried students across the Atlantic on summer work vacations. Leaving the terminal, I ran though the heavy thunder and lightning to the overcrowded plane where chaos reigned. Too many bodies, too much luggage, not enough time to stow everything. The plane trundled down the sodden runway, all lights flickering off for a few unnerving seconds, and then we rose.

I sat nervously in my seat. Where was the parachute? I reached under the seat and groped around hopefully. It hadn't occurred to me that there was no chance of escape if the plane went down. Lightning flashed and thunder rolled amidst the soggy English countryside and we lifted off slowly into the night amidst the bumps and mysterious noises. I was off to a new reality from which, to this day, I have never fully returned.

CHAPTER THREE

∞

THE WAY BEGINS TO OPEN

All across the Atlantic, my ear was attuned to the slightest change in engine noise. Each time it grew quieter, I wondered if the engines were about to fail and we would be plunged into the black ocean below. Throughout the flight I felt an intense trepidation. New York, my first stop, was notorious for its murders, violence, mayhem, and aggressive attitude. This was not going to be a stroll along the Hove promenade.

The plane could only fly as far as Newfoundland, and we landed at Gander to refuel. The worst was now over, it seemed, and it was on to the last leg to JFK Airport, not even seven years after the assassination. On landing, I waited hopefully for the bag that carried all my worldly goods to arrive on the carousel. It was my first flight, and surely the chances of the airline losing my suitcase were small. I waited and waited until finally the forlorn realization dawned that everything I had with me in America had been lost. I was on my own, big time.

When I finally emerged from customs and immigration all the other passengers had long left by charter bus for Manhattan. I walked out to my first glimpse of America on a hot, humid night, and was immediately surrounded by cab drivers offering me different deals, trying to convince me, hustling and bargaining, yelling, cajoling. Wasn't there an established fare? Weren't there meters? Wasn't anybody in charge?

Welcome to America. The sweaty night, competing, accented voices, lack of official guidance, the impossibility of making a good choice with no objective information — it all created an overwhelming impression of a freewheeling, anarchic culture where sharpness of instinct and canny street wisdom were the name of the game. And I was lacking in both.

By the time I arrived in Manhattan at 3:30 AM, my hotel room had been given away and I had no choice but to wander the streets looking for a place to stay. Fortunately, a large, mustachioed Texan in a suit was in the same situation, and he befriended me. There was strength in numbers as we navigated the street grates and their disturbing bursts of steam, the unfamiliar smells, the surprising grime and dirt of the city after a lifetime of images of gleaming skyscrapers. At any moment, I expected a mugger to slip behind us from the doorways. This was not how I had hoped to spend my first night in America.

Arriving in Chicago the next day, I had one contact. Fred was an unpretentious and friendly college guy working as a taxi driver and somehow, when he learned of my plight, he offered me his apartment for a night or two while I found my bearings. It was on the Near North Side of the city, an area filled with Puerto Rican Young Lords, hippies, junkies, and blacks. The neighborhood was funky, humid, and distinctly unglamorous with low, brick houses, broken sidewalks, and ghetto corner stores.

Somehow I got the key to Fred's apartment and let myself in. Directly across the street a huge sign hung from an apartment building reading MEN AGAINST COOL. What on earth did that mean? Why would men be against cool? I had no idea. I thought the whole idea was to be cool. This was definitely a different world.

I felt wary and anxious. I had no idea of the geography of Chicago and this was only a few years after the chaotic and violent Democratic convention when Mayor Daley's cops revealed their thuggery to the world. Just how dangerous was this neighborhood? I wondered.

The Midwestern humid heat in the modest, empty apartment was unbearable to someone used to the cool British climate, and I decided to take a bath, all the time in a state of anxiety that thieves and muggers might break in. While in the bath, I heard a noise in the living room. Oh no! Someone was outside the bathroom door. There were clear noises coming from around the apartment but nobody was saying anything. Had I walked into a nightmare scenario? Was I in deep trouble? "Who's there?" I shouted in the most authoritative tones I could muster while naked, but there was no response. Things were looking grim and I could feel the tension rising in my solar plexus. Maybe America was just too dangerous a place and I should have stayed in good old England.

Just then I heard a scratching at the bathroom door. The dangerous intruder revealed himself — it was Fred's cat, thankfully. America, it seemed, was proving a tense and demanding place.

Chicago had emerged from the violence of the Democratic Convention a year or two earlier but tension hung thick in the air. The Black Panther leader, Fred Hampton, had been gunned down in a hail of bullets while he slept; a Yippie was running for mayor; the Near North Side neighborhood was dominated by Puerto Rican Young Lords trying to merge gang life with social service. The split in American society between advocates of the established order and those demanding change was more intense than ever. Riding the bus to the University down Halsted Street each morning, I noticed the signs. An elderly, white-haired woman got out of her seat next to me and moved three seats ahead rather than sit next to a bearded longhair. She made no effort to conceal her distaste for the likes of me. Driving past the Cabrini Green housing projects every day, we passed a no-go area where police cars were likely to be fired upon by radical black snipers hidden in the towers. I joined an antiwar demonstration in the Loop and was struck by the large number of Vietnam Vets Against the War. Other teaching assistants were taking machine-gun training in Wisconsin on the weekends to prepare for the revolution. The air was thick with tension and hatred, and Nixon was reviled by everyone I knew.

These were the outer trappings of my arrival in America, and the politics of social upheaval gripped me. But underneath, the same old search for meaning continued to pervade my inner life.

It was fascinating to find myself expected to teach the anachronistically entitled Rhetoric 101 at the newly built University of Illinois at Chicago Circle to the sons and daughters of Mayor Daley's blue-collar voters. I had hardened Vietnam vets in the class, black radicals, and just regular Polish kids from the inner city desperately trying to maintain a grade-point average sufficient to avoid the draft. FM alternative radio was in its heyday, and the music was fabulous on the air and in the live clubs. Chicago was a rich stew, a great place to gain a quick understanding of the heart of American culture. It was violent, rowdy, prejudiced, swept by icy winds in winter and sweating with fetid heat in summer, but filled with friendly people delighted to meet someone from Britain.

I went to a blues bar on the North Side of Chicago where Buddy Guy was playing guitar. I remember the rare close intermingling of blacks and whites, the bespectacled Jewish harmonica player, the soulful yells of "Yeah, tell it like it is" from the swaying mass of bodies, all of us feeling every shred of emotion the guitar player expressed. That bar, like so much of Chicago, was rundown, rough at the edges, and slightly squalid, but the vibe and the music were fabulous.

I spent almost a year in Chicago, and it was a serious education in the school of life. I had to learn to be very street-smart. My tutor in this gritty school was my first friend in Chicago, Dennis, a man in his early twenties who had just had himself committed to a mental asylum as the only way to avoid the draft. He had arranged an escape and was now officially a lunatic on the run. I have rarely met a saner person. Thanks to Dennis, I soon came to see that Chicago was a collection of ethnic city-states with distinct borders that you ignored at your peril.

I was hunting for my first apartment and had connected with a fellow teaching assistant, Tom Trombly, a tall, skinny, slow-spoken, ginger-haired hippy from California who had left a commune in the San Fernando Valley to move to Chicago. Tom and I wandered through this old Italian neighborhood with its working-class houses and cracked streets until we found the address we were looking for. We knocked a little hesitantly. Both of us had beards and long hair. An aggressive-looking man in a stained tank top and stubble came to the door and looked us over. Without missing a beat or a breath, he spat, "We don't want no goddamn hippies. Get outta here!" This guy was from central casting. I was so delighted to actually hear the rough accent that had featured in countless gangster movies that I forgave him almost immediately. I'd traveled a long way to be insulted in such a voice, and it didn't feel bad. Welcome to America.

I didn't learn much at the University, but I wasn't there for academic study. I was there to see America in the raw, and that's the education I received. Chicago itself was the school, and I was an eager student looking for life experience, not more books.

But there was one place I really wanted to be as the '60s became the '70s: California. At the first Christmas break, I answered an ad posted on a college wall for a co-driver to Los Angeles. I had always wanted to drive Route 66 ever since reading of the rickety Okie trucks in *The Grapes of Wrath*, and since the first track of the first side of the first Rolling Stones LP: "If you ever plan to motor West, taxi my way / Take the highway that's the best / Get your kicks on Route 66." And so it was off for 2,000 miles, roaring into the Texas sunset at 108 miles per hour, feeling young, alive, and free with a continent filled with infinite scope for adventure opening before me.

My co-driver, Linda, informed me that this would be the best week of my life. She told me she was an astrologer and that the planetary aspects indicated that we were about to have an outrageous experience. I was skeptical but she was cute. Why argue?

Then one December evening at 6,000 feet in the Painted Desert of Arizona, at the site of some fourteenth-century Indian ruins, we both heard the sound of pure silence for the first time. When we stopped the car in the desert and turned off the engine it seemed as though I could hear the Earth revolving though infinite, silent space. The huge vistas of mesa and butte, the landscape on a scale far beyond anything in Western Europe, the enormous, star-packed skies at night, the sense of penetrating the unknown. All these impressions forged a fresh awareness in my twenty-one-year-old psyche. I found myself filled with awe and wonder at the majesty and beauty of these Southwestern desert landscapes, and something in me shifted permanently.

George Harrison's *All Things Must Pass* was just being released as we headed south to Tucson, and we had the chance to spend a week on a ranch in the Santa Catalina Mountains looking south to the Mexican border. We sat on the roof at night, the starlight bursting brilliantly through the desert air. Music of insight and beauty floated up from the record player down below. I could feel something changing within me. I felt I was stepping into a receptive, open way of being in the world, able to be profoundly moved by the colors of the desert mountain peaks at sunset. Somehow, the mix of being twenty-one and entering this vast and holy landscape created the possibility for a new quality of consciousness within me. In these few weeks, in the West, I could feel myself becoming more openhearted, more in love with the world, more deeply awed by natural beauty, and much more aware of the eternal presence of the great silent cosmos. I turned towards the deeper mysteries with a mixture of trepidation and joy, and set my feet towards what I hoped would become a life of deeper meaning.

After the spiritual experience along Route 66, I felt I could never return to a life of graduate school. The world had opened for me in a new way. My time in Brighton had opened the door a crack, but now I had an experience that had lasted a month, and that raised an enormous question for me. If my inner experiences were real, should I devote myself to exploring this new world of spiritual meaning full time?

Many questions lived in my mind. Was a path to enlighten-ment opening, or was I falling into illusion, buying a spiritual worldview when my youth had been characterized by a rejection of established religion and a determination to figure it out for myself? How could I reconcile the intellectual part of me that saw religious teachings as anachronistic with these new experiences that showed me a different way to see the world? How could any honest and perceptive person accept the existence of some kind of higher presence when the whole twentieth century had been a massive accumulation of evidence that life was meaningless, filled with gratuitous horror, and random death?

There was a serious split between my intellectual side and my new mystical experiences. Finding a way to reconcile them, finding the writers who were capable of integrating the two, now became a major factor driving my life.

Life began to change for me at that point. Perhaps a part of myself of which I had been largely unaware was beginning to emerge, stimulated by the desert skies, the empty silences, and perhaps more than anything by the growing sense of a much larger reality around and within me than I had suspected.

Chicago had been an immersion in the darker side of reality with all its inner-city violence, danger, and tension. But it had also provided the opening for me to venture tentatively into an expanded consciousness, and I seized the opportunity. But I needed breathing space, a different environment, and my heart was drawn to the West Coast, where I felt greater openness to the things beginning to move me and guide my life.

I served out my remaining contract as a teaching assistant at the University but my heart wasn't in the studies. Everywhere I looked, I searched for literature that would speak in some way to the spiritual and mystical. And suddenly I was seeing it everywhere. Radhakrishnan's book, *Eastern Religions and Western Thought*, almost fell off the shelf in a bookstore where I was browsing. The first fifty pages spoke exactly to my experiences in the desert.

As 1971 advanced, I felt increasingly clearly that I had to dedicate myself to discovering whether the spiritual experiences I had, and continued to have back in the city, were real. As summer approached I decided to head for the West Coast, modern home of cosmic consciousness, to apply myself fully to esoteric and mystical studies. Staying in the United States was impractical as the Vietnam War still raged. So I headed for British Columbia, Canada to the city of Vancouver. I knew nothing about the place, but had heard that it was beautiful; I felt a tremendous affinity with the West after my journey, with no desire to return to Britain.

But all the way on the road out West, I was worried. How would I make a living? I had very little money and no contacts. Was I leaving a path to education and advancement to pursue a chimera? Could I really trust my inner visions, or were they just hallucinations? Looking back now, I do wonder where I found the courage to head off into the unknown, into a country where I didn't know a soul, with nothing to guide me except a sense that I must respond to my new, inner life. I had never had any kind of career agenda. I could only be guided by the deepest experiences that gripped my psyche. I was twenty-two, and I felt that I had to find out if these elevating experiences were real.

Vancouver turned out to be beautiful but lonely. I knew no one in the whole of Canada and had $130 to my name. I wound up living on a famed hippy block on Seventh Avenue in counter-cultural Kitsilano. There was a sense of community on the street and an openhearted feeling for life and love, but very little intellectual stimulation. Nobody here seemed to read any books. I felt a long, long way from the life of the university and continued to wonder how I could reconcile my spiritual search with my intellectual side.

My meager funds were rapidly disappearing and I had no work permit and no job. I felt profoundly alone. Sitting on the logs on Kitsilano Beach, gazing at the lights of freighters anchored in the harbor, the forested mountains rising at the far side of the bay, I tried to push down the anxiety rising from my solar plexus.

Often I walked around the corner from my small apartment and entered Banyen Books, newly opened in Vancouver after the owner's recent return from India. I found succor and relief reading undisturbed for hours in its incense-filled air, the pictures of holy men and mystics all around, the shelves crammed with books that spoke, in one way or another, to the quest I was now embarked upon. Some of it was occult nonsense, some of it was brilliant, much of it was somewhere in between. I couldn't afford the books but the store had a generous and relaxed policy and, sitting in its spiritually uplifting ambience, I pored over volumes from every spiritual tradition, constantly asking if the opening in consciousness that I had experienced in the desert and after was an authentic glimpse of a deeper reality.

Carl Jung especially came to me at this critical juncture. Night after night, inspired and sustained by my poster of George Harrison on the back of my bedroom door, I devoured Jung. The appearance of similar archetypal figures and images in the dreams of people totally separated by geography and language was a huge factor for me in finding evidence, beyond subjective mystical experience, of a fundamental unity in the world. Jung's insight that our soul is at work in dreams that showed the way toward wholeness by offering wisdom beyond the rational mind was consoling to me, and I soaked up the evidence he offered from the 10,000 dreams he had examined at the Burghölzli clinic.

Jung validated that there really is an element within each of us that is of a transcendent nature. Figures of wisdom could appear in our dream life. Mandalas expressing individuation and the integration of the whole person could be found in the sacred art of many cultures.

Yet we were not simply spiritual beings. We were also possessed of a dark shadow composed of all the repressed and denied aspects of ourselves too uncomfortable for us to face, a dark shadow that could grip us individually or even seize a whole culture or nation. Here was a psychological and spiritual worldview with a sophisticated understanding of evil, something so necessary for me. And the evil within us could be faced and ultimately transmuted if we were honest, brave, and conscious enough to do it.

This was starting to feel like a worldview I could respond to with warmth and affection. I had loved the Indian mystics and psychedelic pioneers, but Jung was grounded in a knowledge of the dark side of the human psyche, and the difficulty of the journey to individuation. Sometimes a writer or artist gives consolation to the soul at just the right moment, and I will always be grateful to Jung for his gift to me at a strained and worrisome time. Now I was starting to feel again that I was on the right track.

Numerous other writers from the mystical and esoteric traditions began to speak directly to my heart. After years of education in which few works aside from fiction really touched my deepest essence, suddenly I was surrounded by writers exactly on my wavelength speaking about the issues that had concerned me since childhood. Here was a rationale for human existence that made sense. I began to see that not only the world's great spiritual traditions, at least in their esoteric forms, spoke of a shared understanding of a higher world, but also many figures from the accepted canon — Blake, Thoreau, Emerson, and Huxley to name a few — knew this secret, and revealed it for the eyes of the awake to see. I began to grasp how a deeper spirituality, beyond established religion, was present even in our secular Western culture, and my long experience of psychic loneliness began to slip away.

When I had moved into my first apartment in Vancouver, shared with a radical Parisian directly involved in the events of '68, I found a solitary paperback book left by the unknown previous occupants on the kitchen sink. It was Doris Lessing's *The Four-Gated City*. It was strengthening to find another writer attuned to intuitive and spiritual insight, and clearly familiar with Jung. I was starting to feel that my decision to explore spiritual truths was paying off. Encounters with books like this helped me feel that life was cooperating in showing me a path forward.

Later that fall a somewhat stoned virtual stranger handed me a book he said he'd had a flash to buy for me. It was Ram Dass' *Be Here Now*, and I sat absorbed night after night making my way through the story of the Harvard professor expelled with Timothy Leary for his experiments with LSD. He had gone to India and actually met his guru, and had written a beautiful, simple, and accessible account of his journey, its revelations, and their relationship to the mystical traditions of the East. This was a narrative and explication of power and significance, as it showed how a searching person could go from psychedelia to disciplined spiritual practice, from dope to *samadhi*, from psychonaut to spiritual teacher. It seemed to hold a key for a whole generation, and I devoured it with joy and delight.

As for George, his influence was inspirational, not intellectual. He was the cool rock star who had also awakened to a mystical reality and whose songs were filled with insights into higher worlds. He made spirituality hip and sexy. It was while listening to "Beware of Darkness" on the *All Things Must Pass* album that I experienced my greatest intuitive knowing of the love that appeared to me the very motor engine of the cosmos.

Meanwhile, life on the physical front was increasingly grim. My meager funds were rapidly disappearing, and the only job I could find was selling copies of one of the first ecological magazines, *The Canadian Conservationist*, door to door. It was a small mom-and-pop operation run from the home of a charming Eastern-European man, and I made a quarter on each sale. I had never sold anything in my life before, and it was wrenching and painful to ring a stranger's door, make a brief pitch, and hope against hope that the door would not be shut in my face. Many a night I walked the dark streets of Kitsilano, often in snow and rain, hoping to emerge with a few dollars for food and rent. And many times I wondered if I had taken a crazy course in my life. Certainly my family back in England felt so, and I had few friends in this cloudy, wet, Northwestern world.

Those nights trudging the streets of Kitsilano were weighing down on me. Too cold, too dark, too poor. I was missing my girl-friend, and in the winter of 1972 I decided to use the return leg of my initial ticket to America to return to England for a visit. Bad move. That winter will go down in my personal annals as close to rock bottom. The relationship was over, complete with enormous pain, and I was reduced to selling velvet paintings door to door in London to make the money to get back to Canada — probably the nadir of this incarnation. I was devastated by the end of the love affair; I was 6,000 miles from where I wanted to be, and I hated London with its foggy, icy weather.

I lived in an apartment in Swiss Cottage with an old friend from university and two other flat-mates. All four of us worked, yet the place was always freezing, there was often no more than one can of baked beans in the fridge, and the only solace was the occasional red glow of a bar from an electric heater. Thankfully, Van Morrison's *Moondance* album had just come out and the foggy horns of "Into the Mystic" sustained me in a time of need. After life on the West Coast, London seemed decades behind the times. The free spirit of the '60s seemed to have disappeared with the Labour government in 1970, and the whole country seemed to me to be depressed, gloomy, and directionless. Of course, it is possible that my own misery just might have contributed to these dire perceptions.

Selling velvet paintings did, however, teach me one valuable lesson. I noticed that I had no courage to do something in which I had no belief. I had to force myself out of that car and up to the front door, whether the garden was "velvet country" (filled with plastic garden gnomes and wagon wheels) or not. I had no inner strength when I tried to do something in which I did not believe. I may have been cold and far from home when I sold *The Canadian Conservationist,* but at least I believed in the value of the magazine. I could hardly say the same thing about the velvet nudes and crude Rembrandt imitations waiting to be hung on suburban London walls.

In London, nobody I knew shared my mystical interests, and my life felt truly rudderless. There were lilac, velvet trousers and high-heeled denim boots for men; there were long, multipronged joints rolled expertly by stoned artists. But I didn't feel the spirit

I was longing for, and I felt adrift. The West Coast called to me with its openness, generosity of spirit, and natural beauty.

When I finally made enough money to catch a plane back to British Columbia in the spring of '72, I left with enormous relief. Flying into Vancouver over the Rockies, I fell into a conversation with a friendly, clean-cut neighbor. He concluded our chat by informing me that Canada needed people like me. It was a gracious welcome. When I turned up at the basement apartment of Gary, a friend from my prior stay, he wasn't there and I made myself at home in that relaxed way of the time. When he did show up a few hours later, he seemed barely to have noticed that I'd been gone for four long, endless months.

It was springtime in British Columbia and nature was resplendent. The sun shone most days, unlike the depressing rainy days in London, and I slipped back into the counterculture with joy. I got a job as an emergency night inspector for the Canadian SPCA, saving animals injured in car accidents if I could, and killing them mercifully if they were dying. I made a lot of life-and-death decisions during those months, and reluctantly killed too many living creatures. In the system of that time, there was no alternative, and I could only try to do it with compassion. But even that job was more tolerable than selling velvet paintings door to door in the cold and damp. Almost anything was.

One evening I saw a show on Machu Picchu and was gripped by its aura of mystery. It seemed to symbolize some kind of lost wisdom hidden, unnoticed until the early twentieth century in the heart of the Andes. Ever since I had read *Exploration Fawcett* as a boy I had wanted to go to South America. And since the age of sixteen, I had always had the urge to hitchhike until the end of the road, to keep on going until there was nowhere to go. I wanted to see those mysterious pyramids in Mexico and Central America about which my education had told me nothing. I suspected that evidence of mysteries from ancient cultures was still all around us, and I needed to see it for myself. Besides, no one I knew had traveled south of Mexico, except for one nine-year-old boy and his hippy mum who had driven to Guatemala and back in an old VW bus.

I had managed to accumulate $640 through my part-time work — enough, I thought, to get me to Machu Picchu and back with a bit of luck. On January 3, 1973, on a snowy Vancouver night, I said goodbye to my friends, got into the back of a van driven by Canada's only self-employed deaf mute, stretched out on a foam mattress covering the floor, looked across at Jeannie, my traveling companion, and kissed the comfortable world of BC goodbye. I had no idea it would be fifteen years before I returned.

CHAPTER FOUR

∞

HITCHHIKING TO MACHU PICCHU AND BEYOND

Something in me wanted to know adventure and freedom, to explore ancient and forgotten cultures and glimpse the mysteries they held, to travel where no one I knew had ever gone before. At the age of ten I had read Colonel P. H. Fawcett's incredible tales of South America in the early twentieth century collected posthumously in that epic work, *Exploration Fawcett*. The forty-foot anacondas and thatched-roof huts filled with nests of poisonous spiders had seized my imagination and, apparently, I had assured my parents that I was off to South America at the earliest opportunity.

In the early '70s, young travelers in Latin America carried worn copies of Carlos Castaneda and were on the lookout for men of knowledge and power in the indigenous nations they encountered. We had P. D. Ouspensky's *In Search of the Miraculous* and the bibliography from the back of Ram Dass' *Be Here Now* in our backpacks and an insatiable desire to find places of ancient mystery and magic. But for me, Central Asia and India were no longer the destination of choice. By 1973, the old hippy trail overland through Turkey and Afghanistan to India had been done and, it seemed to me, was beginning to appear a bit overdone. I wanted somewhere largely unexplored by countercultural vagabonds: a genuine journey into the unknown.

And that is certainly what I found. After days of travel down the West Coast, we crossed the border at night in Mexicali. Seated in the back of a van, my banned long hair hidden under a woolen cap, we passed the ranging flashlights of the Mexican border police, turned a corner, and within one block found ourselves in another world. The well-lit, antiseptic buildings of Southern California were suddenly replaced by darkened, dusty roads; anarchic, brightly lit stores where everything was piled at random; people milling everywhere on the sidewalks; old cars veering in seemingly random directions, barely functional streetlights; strolling mariachi bands; and, from the looks of the women, hints of a dark, intense eroticism. Welcome to Latin America!

The deserts and dry mountains seemed to go on forever as we journeyed south. How could anyone live in such aridity and poverty? But then I remembered Castaneda's Don Juan and his remark that young Yaqui people, no matter how impoverished, always had the chance to become men or women of knowledge, something denied the majority of infinitely wealthier Americans.

I certainly didn't know that the world's greatest pyramids were in Mexico, not Egypt. Standing atop the Pyramid of the Sun in Teotihuacan outside Mexico City I was struck by how these great monuments had already been "ancient" by the time the Aztecs arrived. What forgotten concepts had motivated this lost culture to construct such an otherworldly environment? Why was so little attention paid to these distant cultures by those who proudly proclaimed their grasp of human history and evolution? Surrounded by the old Toltec mysteries, I felt again the need to search for lost knowledge. To me those pyramids stood as symbols of the mystery at the heart of life that had long been neglected.

By the time we reached Oaxaca, we were in a mostly Indian world. An increased sense of mystery hung in the air. The girth and presence of the aged Tule tree, said to be the center of the world by the Maya, was deeply impressive. Standing under the shade of its boughs in the hot sun I could sense the millennia of spiritually attuned cultures that had found inspiration in its presence and beauty, and felt the absolute spiritual centrality of nature in the native philosophy of the Western Hemisphere.

But it was when we saw the mountains of Guatemala in the distance that magic really began to take hold. Swathed in mists, rising up from its surroundings like a lost world or a Central American Tibet, this land looked like something from another time. The military, bristling with guns, were everywhere. Yet the native Mayan people, who comprised the majority of the population, were so graceful and beautiful — the women in their gorgeous, embroidered shirts; the men with their quiet, dignified air. There was both an atmosphere of deep peace engendered by the natural beauty of the land and a feeling of military menace.

I turned twenty-four in the Mayan jungle city of Tikal on the night of the full moon and suddenly felt very old, perhaps older than I have ever felt at a birthday since. Maybe it was the recognition that I was no longer a teenager, but something in me felt ancient. Perhaps impressed by the ornamented males of native cultures, I decided to mark the occasion by having my left ear pierced at midnight on top of the Jaguar Temple. Somehow a clothespin was produced to numb my ear, plus rubbing alcohol, and even a few pieces of ice. But a thunderous downpour that lasted all night meant that fate decreed otherwise, saving me from the dark jungle with the coral snakes and poisonous spiders of my fervid imagination.

Later in Belize City I walked through the shanties on the main river and met Professor Razzle-dazzle, Big Dee, and the unforgettable and enormous Miss Chrissy, owner of the combined bar, boxing gym, and bordello where I wound up staying. Beneath the blazing gold and scarlet sunset, the low bass beat of reggae music was everywhere, joints were sold for a dollar at a seaside bar, and whatever problem you had, someone on the street assured you they could fix it.

Later, sailing leisurely back to the mainland from the island cays under a vast, multihued sky, watching playful dolphins dart, our legs dangling in the warm Caribbean waters, everything seemed at peace. These were the clear, turquoise seas and warm tropical breezes I had longed for so much of my life during the harsh, windswept nights of foggy Pennine England. Belize was a break from the dark, deep, mythological world of Latin America. Its simple charm and friendly English-speaking people were such a sweet surprise.

Back in Guatemala, again I had the urge to do something really wild. I decided to hitchhike down the Río de la Pasión, a remote river than ran, as far as I could tell, vaguely back in the direction of Guatemala City. In a dusty little river town I found a fisherman and his son who were willing to give us a ride in their outboard motor–propelled canoe. For two baking days, we journeyed through endless jungle until finally they concluded they had to turn back. Water levels were unusually low, and there was simply not enough water for them to continue south. These kind and gracious men dropped us off at a one-man finca on the river-bank and wished us luck in our onward journey. And there we were, literally in the middle of nowhere. Our host was amazed to see us but generous with the beans and corn he grew on his small plot. A shy and gracious man, he lived alone with his skinny and mangy dog for company, and his rifle. For scorching day after scorching day I listened for the sound of a canoe engine on the river. At night, I tossed on the hard ground of a simple bamboo hut trying not to think about snakes and how easily they could get into your sleeping bag. I pulled mine up really tight despite the tremendous heat. I became attuned to the faintest engine-like sounds but they would always turn out to be a plane high above us. Many times I thought we were doomed to never get out of this godforsaken spot.

And then one day a big canoe appeared around a bend in the river with a government inspector on board making his annual tour of inspection. I couldn't believe our luck and we leaped, joyful and relieved, into his canoe. Then for days we climbed treacherous rapid after rapid. At each one, there would be a narrow channel a few feet wide through which the water poured against us. Our helmsman would point the boat head-on into this huge surge of water and rev the outboard motor to the max. This would bring us to a precarious point of balance in which the power of the engine matched equally the force of the river. At this point most of the men in the boat would leap to their feet; run agilely with perfect balance down the narrow side of the wooden canoe; each grab a long pole; and, with huge effort, shove the boat past the critical point, thus averting for another hour the possibility of our whole cargo winding up on the riverbed, quite possibly along with a few of us.

Throughout the struggle with each rapid, our Mayan helmsman remained imperturbable with his easy smile usually visible under his big straw hat. Our fellow passengers, mostly Indians, spoke in a language that had more clicking sounds than words, and their Spanish was meager to nonexistent. They were invariably gracious to these weird light-skinned strangers. I have often wondered since what happened to those humble people in the holocaust inflicted by the Guatemalan army that began not many years later.

After ten days on the river, we reached our destination. This was the most remote experience I had known, and I was grateful for the sense of distance from the madness of civilization. I was happy to leave roads, villages, and beds behind to see into another reality of native people, canoes, jungle birds, and other animals. These moments of stepping away from the material world were essential for me to find a sane worldview. It is when life achieves its greatest simplicity that the clearest values arise in our hearts.

Now it was time to head for El Salvador, the most over-populated country in Latin America. After the silence and beauty of Guatemala, the overcrowded, fetid city was hard to take. The sight of a longhaired male was still enough to turn the heads of whole buses, and everything seemed hopelessly crammed together and chaotic. Near the border with Honduras, I learned that a recent war had been fought between Honduras and El Salvador over a soccer game. Best not to stick around. In Nicaragua, the results of a huge earthquake were still visible, and the inner part of Managua was sealed off by barbed wire from potential looters. At the border of Costa Rica, the otherwise friendly immigration officer informed me that long hair was for women and homo-sexuals, and that I must cut mine to a manly length right now if I wished to enter his country. He handed me a pair of scissors and pointed to the bathroom. I was furious, having made my way by this time through many borders manned by men with a very hostile view of longhairs. But as the only alternative was to back-track through an earthquake-devastated land I reluctantly agreed, only to find in the capital city, San José, that Costa Rica was by far the most Americanized of Central American countries and that long male hair was everywhere.

We were getting close to South America, and I was starting to feel its pull. Jeannie, my auburn-haired, gutsy, and adventurous traveling companion from Vancouver, decided that she had gone as far as she wished to go and opted to stay in Central America. The time had come for us to part and we both felt it. I waved one last time as I walked alone down the railroad tracks through the high ferns outside Puerto Limón on the Caribbean coast, over the small wooden bridge that spanned the river, and boarded the slow train back up into the mountains.

On May 1, I boarded a plane to Cartagena, Colombia. At the airport I noticed a copy of the *International Herald Tribune*. Its cover photo was of Haldeman and Ehrlichman standing together in dark glasses and raincoats, looking insidious and conspiratorial. Nixon was about to throw them to the wolves, and as I boarded the plane, one thing was clear: The times they were a-changin'.

★ ★ ★ ★ ★

Most young males have the impulse to push themselves to the limit, to test their capacities. For my father and grandfather's generations, they had no choice but to find their tests in the trenches of the Somme or the fields and towns of Normandy and Nazi-occupied Holland. For many of my age in America, Vietnam, or the struggles against the war, pushed them to find parts of themselves of which they had been unaware. For me, this time of youthful testing was South America.

There is nothing in Central America to prepare you for Colombia. After months of easygoing people, mostly poor but friendly, Barranquilla was a very rude shock. An air of menace seemed to hang over. It seemed that life was cheap, and blood flowed easily.

A few days after arriving, while attempting to travel from Santa Marta to Cartagena, my bus broke down in the hardcore slums of Barranquilla, and it was every man for himself. I was the only foreigner on board and, instead of trying to flag down a taxi and heading for somewhere vaguely safe, I was in money-saving mode and tried to make my way on foot to a bus stop. Unfortunately, a gang of destitute youths was in the way.

This was the only time in my life I have known a direct physical attack with a broken bottle. Set upon by two men at night in a neglected, rubbish-strewn public park, there was no appeal to reason. One of them had a maniacal strength born of some kind of derangement. When he tried to get his bottle edge near my throat, I forgot all notions of fair fighting. I grabbed the bastard's hair and pulled it viciously with all the strength I could muster. This was enough for him to let go his iron grip on my neck and I broke from their grasp. Deciding that the sleeping bag and clothes in my backpack were not enough to die for, I used the fleetness of foot developed by years of cross-country running and headed for the streetlights and a group of people, yelling loudly, "*Ladrones, ladrones,*" the only word I could remember in Spanish for thieves.

My hands were cut up a little, but the shock was so intense I didn't know if I was cut nastily on the face or not. I still had my faithful leather jacket, complete with passport and $240 worth of traveler's checks. I found an all-night emergency clinic where they patched me up and assured me I didn't need stitches. Briefly I pondered whether enough was enough and maybe I should head back to the safety of North America. I was deeply shocked and upset, but I wasn't going to let this deter me from reaching Machu Picchu. I bought a couple of cheap cotton shirts and a towel, put them in a ten-cent straw bag, and headed south. It seemed that hitchhiking was not advisable in this crazy place; besides, the rickety buses were so cheap that you could cross the length of Colombia for about ten dollars. As the bus rolled inland from the coast, I began to see the outlines of the Andes and my heart soared. Outside Medellin, the war with the guerillas was happening in earnest. All males were taken off the bus, lined up at gunpoint, and searched closely for weapons. In the city itself, I had my first encounters with Colombian bar life with its scantily clad, flirtatious women who emanated an intense sexuality that was both attractive and mysterious.

After Cali, the mountains became higher, more severe, and colder. I knew nobody who had ever been this way before, and my only preparation was reading Prescott's marvelous *History of the Conquest of Peru*, a tale of vicious thuggery by the conquistadors in the face of a highly developed culture. As I began to hear the otherworldly clicking sounds of the Quechua tongue, my mind turned often to the forgotten world of the Incas that had stimulated my whole trip. By the time I reached Pasto near the border, the nights had become icy and star-filled. Rattling down the mountainsides in an old bus missing half its windows, my leather jacket pulled close around me, my feet bare but for sandals after months of tropical warmth, I shivered uncontrollably. The Andes stretched away into the distance in silent vastness.

During ten days crossing Colombia, I had met only three foreigners. What would Ecuador hold? At 10,000 feet, I was entering a new world. The ubiquitous presence of DAS, the corrupt Colombian secret police always on the lookout to extort money for some minor violation, fell away. Ecuador seemed much more peaceful and sane. My funds were running very low and I still had to get to Machu Picchu and back. Should I try hitchhiking again?

I turned a corner in the border town of Ipiales and encountered a sight I had never seen before in South America: A tall blond guy with John Lennon glasses, a plaid shirt, cowboy boots, and a ponytail alongside a small, intense, dark-haired woman standing by the side of the dirt road, both with their thumbs out at passing vehicles. "*Por favor, atrás. Porque no?*" the man shouted in execrable Spanish as he gesticulated wildly at each truck rumbling by.

Who on earth was this? These people looked as crazy as me. I walked up to them and learned that he was Californian, she Colombian, and they were heading for Peru. We had barely begun our conversation when a pickup truck suddenly pulled over. "Wanna hit it?" Cliff said.

49

"Sure. Why not?" I shrugged and clambered into the back of the truck with the two of them. And thus began a saga that lasted for thousands of miles.

Cliff had a beard, baggy jeans, and was carrying a hidden machete in his big orange pack. Leda was pale skinned with jet-black hair, dressed in a polo-necked sweater and white trousers. That day was the fulfillment of a hitchhiking dream. The truck teetered along winding mountain roads, crossing crumbling bridges over chasms, enormous snow-capped mountains above us. This seemed high adventure, heading into the unknown, a spirit of exhilaration infusing my soul after the danger and stress of Colombia. I stood in the back of the truck, the wind blowing my hair wildly, epic vistas opening up with each turn of the road, and felt fully alive. Yeah, *this* was living; this was free and adventurous and fun.

In Quito, the Ecuadorian capital, we rested a little, and then began the longest hitchhiking run of my life to reach the capital of Peru. We hitched a ride in a big truck to Guayaquil, the sleazy Pacific port. Standing at night at a truck stop outside the city in the humid, polluted tropical air, the vast container trucks moving out of the port and heading into the darkness, it looked like it was going to be a night at the side of the road for us. But Leda, with her flirtatious charm, convinced a trucker to open the back of his empty vehicle and let us in. I will always remember the booming, echoing sound of the sledgehammer as the driver sealed us into this huge, empty container coffin and we rumbled into the night toward who knows where. Sitting on the floor in pitch darkness, every whine of the brakes shrieked and howled through this gigantic echo chamber. Vehicles coming up behind sent long laser beams of light through the cracks in the rear door, creating a bizarre sound-and-light show. Rolling through the night in a blackness filled with otherworldly howls and strange light formations, Cliff revealed his capacity to see the light side of things. "Maybe we came here to die," he confided.

Somehow we traveled through the night, all through the next day, and then a second night in the Atacama Desert. I had never imagined that deserts would be cold at night, but this was freezing and we were glad to arrive in fog-shrouded Lima. There was nothing romantic about this place. It seemed permanently wrapped in chilly, gray mist; a depressed aura hung over the whole city. So *this* was the long-awaited Peru? We left rapidly and headed into the mountains towards Cuzco. Passing the snow line, still without sweater or socks, I realized I was reaching the heart of the Andes. In Ayacucho, I bought for a few dollars a brown, llama-wool poncho, thick socks, and a hat with earflaps. There was little to suggest that this would become the future scene of numerous violent acts by the *Sendero Luminoso*, the Shining Path guerillas. Now the sky was becoming huge and the mountains increasingly vast. For days we journeyed through tiny villages where the cemeteries were much grander than the homes. In those days you only heard that evocative Andean pipe music in the Andes themselves, and each note took me deeper into a mysteriously beautiful world.

At last we rumbled down our final, brown-and-gray mountainside into Cuzco, ancient capital of the Incas. Nobody imagined then that it would become the South American Kathmandu within twenty years, but it had an immediately impressive and mysterious air. The fortress of Sacsayhuaman high above the town confirmed all one's suspicions that something extraordinary had happened here. Vast irregularly shaped rocks fit together so closely that you could not get a razor blade between them. I read that the Peruvian army had been unable to raise even one of these massive blocks with all the benefits of modern technology, and yet here were thousands of them fitted together impeccably. Had the modern world wiped out some body of ancient knowledge?

Determined to make it to Machu Picchu the cheapest and most mystical way possible, we decided to hitch up the Valley

51

of the Incas. In the small village of Písac, below a mountainside covered in ancient graves, I witnessed a too-common tragedy of mountain life. The narrow dirt roads of the Andes constitute the world's most hair-raising land travel: terrifying drops and insufficient room for two vehicles to pass. When trucks and buses met, one vehicle often had to back up with its wheels only inches from the edge of the cliff. In these mountains you chose your driver very carefully. You saw upturned trucks thousands of feet below the road in riverbeds, the result of momentary poor judgment or sheer bad luck. While in Písac, I began to hear loud wailing and weeping. Women were crying and running through the center of the village. A truck carrying a large number of the village men had gone over a cliff and killed everyone on board. How do you respond to a tragedy like this? It seemed the latest in a long line of events that have battered these stoic people since the shameless and brutal destruction of their high culture by Francisco Pizarro and his gold-obsessed thugs in the sixteenth century.

Later, hitchhiking up the Sacred Valley of the Incas, surrounded by beauty, I felt free and alive. I was walking at dusk in the midst of mysteries into the unknown, with no certainty of a bed for that night. How far was the next town? Magic was in the air amidst the towering snowcaps, and the laughter in the eyes of the Indian women who wore high, white hats and spoke with clicking tongues.

Boarding a train from Ollantaytambo for the last hour or two to the sacred city itself I felt the intense exhilaration of almost reaching my destination. We climbed off by the railroad tracks. A small fleet of minibuses provided transport for the wealthy staying in the tourist hotel at the top of the mountain, but for the likes of us, there were a few wooden shacks with crude pallets made of tree branches by the side of the river. We dropped off our few possessions and headed up the steep mountainside by a small path. It was a demanding climb, but I was so excited that

I had boundless energy. It was easy to see why this place was not discovered until 1911. As we got closer to the summit, the landscape began to open up and silent grandeur began to take hold of us. Finally, at the summit, we gazed on the ancient ruins. Above us, on the opposite peak, the Temple of the Moon; before us, the Temple of the Sun. For decades archeologists had mistakenly considered this some kind of fortress. It was clear that this was a deeply holy place.

There were few visitors and they left soon. Before long, we stood pretty much alone at the hitching post of the sun at 8,000 feet. The green and brown slopes of the mountains all around us swept down to the river as it made its U-shaped curve around the sacred mountain. As evening approached, the mantle of clouds above us and the higher mountains all around formed a vast, perfect natural amphitheater with a lilac-colored dome. A profound silence settled. The only sound was the distant rushing of the Urubamba River thousands of feet below us. We stood transfixed in the spiritual heart of the Andes, our souls gripped by an overwhelming sense of awe and wonder. As dusk began to gather, flashes of lightning outlined the Temple of the Moon on the peak opposite us.

Weren't there also other natural holy places where a mysterious combination of landscape elements and some subtle presence produced a profound feeling of reverence among sensitive people? Perhaps ancient cultures had possessed a consciousness of this that we had mostly lost. As I gazed out on this vision of sublime beauty, I knew intuitively that there were many other spots on the planet where this feeling of magical reverence was generated organically.

Those moments at Machu Picchu have stayed with me as glimpses of a deeper order beneath the surface of life. I felt a quiet humility in the face of those ancient Incan secrets, and a longing to see into the mysteries of existence with a wisdom similar to that which had clearly inspired the priests. I felt I was granted a moment of insight into divine harmonies inaccessible to the five senses, and was truly grateful. This was the apex of my pilgrimage, and I had received something unexpected — a taste of inner peace that has remained with me all my life, and a glimpse of the sacred places of the earth where the old mysteries had been celebrated. I could ask for nothing more.

We could not drag ourselves away from this transcendent scene, but as darkness had crept upon us, it was unclear how we would find our way down the mountain paths. Arm in arm so as not to lose contact we stumbled downward in the darkness, silent lightning flashes occasionally illuminating the winding track and throwing the Temple of the Moon into dramatic relief high above us. At last, we found our way to the huts where we had left our possessions, and threw ourselves down on those primitive cots. It was bitterly cold and, wrapped in my poncho, I tossed all night trying vainly to sleep.

We left the following morning on the train. The visit had been brief but perfect. Now that the object of my adventure had been accomplished, there remained the knotty problem of how to return to North America with my meager funds. Still the Andes beckoned. Surely I couldn't head back without seeing Lake Titicaca and maybe even Bolivia. After a night or two in Cuzco, we determined to hitch for the lake. Little did I know that I was about to experience the coldest night of my life.

In some remote village, notable only for the hostility of its inhabitants to any "gringos," we flagged down a potato truck and after some hesitation climbed on top. There we found a handful of Indians atop the potato sacks. The slow-moving truck lumbered on and the temperatures fell lower and lower. By the time we reached a high pass I was shivering uncontrollably. The zip on my trusty leather jacket broke and I could only huddle with my poncho wrapped around my feet, still suffering the ill effects of a mutton soup given us the night before in which the lumps of meat still had wool attached to them. The driver stopped at one point to pull back that tarp to prevent the potatoes from freezing, not to protect us. My fingernails cracked and began to bleed. There was no heat anywhere in my body, no ability to revive warmth by blowing on my hands or rubbing any body part; warmth had disappeared totally. We stopped to ford a river under the clear night sky. It was bitter, bitter cold.

The night went on, with endless, futile attempts to find a comfortable body position and sleep. By the time sunrise came, we had reached Lake Titicaca, and I was close to suffering from exposure. We pulled into the lakeside town of Juliaca and climbed stiffly down from the top of the truck in the early-morning sunlight. I shivered violently for the next few hours. But there was this amazing lake, stretching endlessly before us like a huge inland sea. The sun was well up before we stopped shaking, and the night seemed no more than a nightmare. Had it been real?

On the far side lay Bolivia, a land where three quarters of the people were indigenous, the Tibet of South America, somewhere truly off the beaten path at that time. I couldn't resist. A truck ride across the Bolivian border was the small town of Copacabana, where we decided to spend the night. Here a hill rose above the lake from which the small Islands of the Sun and the Moon — the legendary birthplace of the Incan gods — were visible.

The following afternoon I climbed the nearest hillside to gaze down upon the great lake. All afternoon I sat silently on the hilltop watching the shades of Lake Titicaca turn from green to blue to indigo while scarlet clouds hung on distant mountaintops. My being was filled with an almost inexplicable sense of wholeness. My heart was full, my mind at peace, my body at rest after long exertions. But there was something more than that. Again I had the sense of being at a sacred spot, somewhere where the harmonies of Heaven and Earth were more perceptible. As I descended the hill at dusk, I had a deep sense that this feeling was why I had come so far. There was no obvious source of such satisfaction, but for hours as I gazed on those mystical waters, I had been filled with a transcendent serenity.

I had done it. I had made it to my goal, all the way from Canada, and this was my first opportunity to rest and consider after the rush of leaving the sacred city, and the agonies of the journey out of Peru. I had endured many a crisis to be sitting overlooking that wondrous lake. I felt mature and capable of facing the world. I simply sat and sat. I did not consciously meditate. I walked down to the village at dusk with the clear feeling: *This is why I came to South America.*

Now we were ready for the capital, and hitched a ride in an open truck with Aymara Indians, each with his cheek bulging with a wad of coca leaves. The truck stopped to ford a shallow river and we found ourselves facing a group of goose-stepping, black-shirted marines. Posters of the dictator, Hugo Banzer, with his disturbing little moustache, were starting to appear everywhere. A soldier climbed the sides of our truck to inspect us. When he saw us, his eyes widened, and he spat one word — "Heepies!" — with a look of contempt. I suppose my headband and beard didn't help.

The empty plains seemed to go on forever; suddenly we turned sharp left and dropped steeply. A huge crater appeared in the earth. There was a large city far, far below, as if at the bottom of the Grand Canyon. It was late afternoon, and the reflected pink rays from the enormous snowcap Illimani that rises above La Paz cast a beautiful if melancholic glow across the whole basin.

I had the desire to cross the Andes all the way to the savannah country in the east of Bolivia. We hitched across the Altiplano to the old silver town of Oruro, and the following morning landed a ride in a long flatbed truck all the way to Cochabamba, sixteen hours to the east. This journey stands in my memory as the most exhilarating ride I ever took. The truck passed a broken-down wooden sign reading 5,000 METRES, meaning that we were approaching 16,000 feet. Sitting amongst pipes in the back of the truck, huddled together for warmth under our ponchos, we could see great condors flying high in the sky. Snowcapped peaks seemed to go on to infinity all around us. I had never felt so full, so able to see so far, so awed by the size and beauty of the world.

By the time night fell, we were under a brilliant starry canopy. That same deep love of the stars that I had experienced in Tucson three years earlier came back to me. How, I wondered, could anybody imagine that we mere human beings, on our tiny planet in this vast cosmos, have figured out the ultimate nature of reality? Beneath a brilliant night sky high in the world's greatest mountains, it was difficult to take the certainties of scientific materialism seriously. How could we know, a mere 200 years after the rise of modern technology, that only the sense-perceptible world is real? It seemed shortsighted, to say the least.

Then it was time to head for Santa Cruz province, where Che Guevara had been killed six years previously. As we reviewed the various trucks about to set off in our direction, I knew this would be another hair-raising ride. I examined each driver very carefully to see who seemed the most sane, balanced, and sober. We made our choice, hopped in the back of the truck, and headed off. After a long, long ride, we began to feel the altitude dropping and a feeling of warmth in the evening air. This felt so foreign after months of icy cold at night ever since the mountains in the far south of Colombia.

This was the southernmost point of the journey. Now it was time to head north to Colombia; from there, fly to Miami, and then hitchhike to British Columbia. Leaving Lake Titicaca for the coast, we hitched a ride in the back of a pickup truck. Descending from the high Andes in an endless series of hairpin bends, I lay in the back of the truck, breathing that familiar South American mix of gasoline fumes and cold dust, trying to fight off nausea.

When at last we arrived in the city of Arequipa at about 4,000 feet, it felt like I had returned to "civilization" as commonly understood. As we approached the city, I could see industrial chimneys belching smoke. The faces of the residents seemed strained after the serenity of the Indian faces with which I had become familiar. That night I went to a movie theater for the first time in many months to see Paul Newman in *WUSA*, a film about a radio station in New Orleans. I remember nothing about the plot. What struck me with appalling force was the contorted expressions on the characters' faces. Their anxieties had made them exceptionally ugly, or so it seemed to me after my mountain sojourn.

The whole experience of returning to modern urban life produced in me an overwhelming sensation that Western civilization was destroying both the Earth and the souls of its inhabitants. From the obscenely grim factories to the pinched, fearful, angry faces of the people, it was clear that this modern world of industry and profit that had so much of the planet in its grip was fundamentally out of balance with the universe. Right down to the deepest core of my being, I felt this truth. The world today must be restored to health and well-being.

I did not set out on a self-conscious vision quest in going to South America, but I had inadvertently experienced one. I knew from that point on that my life's work needed to be about restoring wholeness to the human spirit and to the natural environment.

At Machu Picchu and Lake Titicaca, I had tasted insight into the sacred dimensions of the world. Now I saw with piercing intuitive clarity how this forgotten sense of harmony with the cosmos must be restored if we are to have a viable future. In a sense, the goal of the journey had been accomplished. I would return a changed man.

North America beckoned. In Lima, everything depended on maximizing my paltry financial resources. My Colombian friend and co-traveler, Leda, went out one day to the black marketeers to change into dollars the little money left from the various currencies acquired since the border of Ecuador months before. Then she disappeared. Cliff had remained in La Paz, and for two days I paced and wondered and worried. At six o'clock in the morning there was a knock on the door of my cheap little hotel near the Presidential palace. I answered with some trepidation. There was Leda. She looked at me and I could see tears in her eyes. "*Ay, yo he perdido toda la plata*," she moaned. She had lost all the money and been harassed relentlessly by the police for days simply because she was Colombian.

By a stroke of good fortune, I happened to have two twenty-dollar bills in my jeans pocket. I was 6,000 miles from home. Now it was really time to return. The only question was how.

∽

CHAPTER FIVE

ON THE EDGE IN COLOMBIA AND CALIFORNIA

COLOMBIA

The Atacama Desert is the driest place in the world. It hasn't rained there in recorded history, and the remains of ancient civilizations are mummified perfectly by the dry, hot air. I gazed out at the Pacific Ocean as I stood by the side of the Pan-American Highway waiting for the next ride north to Ecuador. The six-dollar bus ticket I had been required to purchase to enter Peru had taken me fifty or sixty miles south of the border, and now I had to make my own way back north.

Grizzled old farmers with flatbed trucks carried me for five or ten kilometers and then left me to my next ride. But the sun was warm, the ocean serene. I lit up my last smoke and inhaled quietly as I waited for the next ramshackle vehicle, my straw bag by my side, my brown-and-white llama-wool poncho rolled up and tied with rope hanging from my shoulder, my scuffed old leather jacket fending off breezes from the chilly Pacific current. I couldn't escape a dose of anxiety: I had less than forty dollars. Who knew how much the immigration officers in Ecuador would require? Would they even let me in?

As we arrived in the border town, it felt more like the Caribbean than Peru. In the sun-washed alleys, children ran shouting, tropical music was blaring, and an atmosphere of mellow neglect permeated the whole place. I found the Ecuadorian immigration office and walked hesitantly through the door. At the end of a long room, two very official, stern gentlemen sat behind wooden desks glaring curiously at me. This could be difficult. The two twenty-dollar bills in my jeans pocket were the sum of my worldly goods. Would I be able to talk them into letting me into the country?

As I made my way towards them, a song suddenly burst through the row of open windows. The salsa disappeared, and the soaring slide guitar of George Harrison sounded sweetly in the dry warmth: "Give me peace on earth / Give me light, give me life / Keep me free from birth / Give me hope, help me cope with this heavy load / Trying to touch and reach you with heart and soul." It seemed like a blessing and my heart lifted.

The immigration officer eyed me warily. With my long hair, goatee, coral necklace, and faded jeans, I wasn't the typical person crossing the border on foot. But that dose of George mellowed me, let me access humor and reserves of charm. The officer began to try a little basic English and I began to tutor him on a few phrases. Before long, we were smiling and pronouncing phrases together. When he finally asked me how much time I wanted in his country and how much money I had, the little white lie of $400 slipped effortlessly from my lips and was accepted without question. He stamped my passport for two months, we shook hands warmly, and I headed for the door with a sigh of relief.

Now I was headed back north into the mountains. Wrapped in my poncho, long wool socks under my *huaraches*, I felt again the silence and stillness of the Andes. We rose higher and higher into the vast darkness, the sense of silent, empty, brooding mountains around us.

I had been out of touch with my family for months and on arriving in Quito, I headed to the British embassy to pick up my mail. On the street that housed the embassy, I noticed a small guy with very long hair and a few days' stubble walking alone and looking bemused.

His name was Paul. A former amateur boxer and taxi driver from Manchester, he had hitchhiked from Turkey to India, spent a year in Australia, and was now making his way back to Britain from New Zealand by boat. He had left the ship in Panama and headed into South America just to get a taste of yet another exotic part of the planet. He sounded like my kind of guy.

We hatched a plan to visit a tiny spa town known appropriately as Baños that lay at the foot of the Tungurahua volcano, near the entry to the Amazon basin. One night I stayed at an Australian hippy doctor's hut on the edge of town that was infested by rats and fleas. After a sleepless night, I found myself covered in nasty, horribly itchy bites. Within a week, these had become infected, and antibiotic creams achieved nothing. With no alternative, I turned to the skills of the local *bruja*, or medicine woman, to whom I was introduced by a renegade Chicago businessman on the run from the law. An intelligent and focused woman with a sensible and efficient air, she quickly diagnosed the problem, brewing up a delightful concoction with clear instructions to drink it with regularity. It had an orangey taste. Her presence inspired trust; within five days, the infection was gone, and I found myself deeply impressed by the effectiveness of indigenous medicine. This important awakening opened my mind to the power of natural cures and deepened my respect for the knowledge of native peoples.

Returning to Quito, my meager funds were almost gone, and my visa was about to expire. It was impossible to stay in peaceful Ecuador due to immigration restrictions resulting from the brutal coup in Chile and the flight north of many Chileans. Unfortunately, there was no alternative to hitchhiking to Colombia.

On the morning of my departure, I awoke after a restless and sick night with a splitting headache, pains in every joint in my body, and a general sense of exhaustion and debility. Great! It was the last day of my visa, and I had to go even though I could barely put one foot ahead of the other. I stumbled toward the exit of the primitive yoga camp where I had been staying, sick and worried.

The road from Quito to the border led through sweaty jungles, windswept mountains, heat, and sheets of icy rain, past strange, African-like villages in the depths of the valley and tiny Indian mountain hamlets. I stood forlornly by the roadside as rain poured down from the mountains with my thumb out, cold, wet, sick, and exhausted. What was wrong with me? I had no idea. All I knew was that I had never felt so bad in my life, but I had to get to the border before fines began for overstaying my visa.

It was a long, grim, nauseating day. I felt weak, lonely, and worried. Gradually we made our way in trucks and vans toward the border. Night was beginning to fall when we hitched our last ride in a big-wheeled truck going to Colombia. With a sigh of relief, I hauled myself into the cab. At least I'd make the border while my visa was still good. Now it was time to head for Bogotá and some kind of job that would help me generate the money to return to North America. But the sickness only grew worse. Stumbling through the rain-swept streets of Pasto, the icy down-pour soaking my rope sandals and freezing my feet, the nausea welled up with increasing frequency.

We headed for San Agustín, site of some of the most impressive pre-Columbian ruins in the country and well-established hippy central for Colombian counterculture. By the time we arrived, my eyes had started to go yellow. Paul, veteran traveler that he was, diagnosed the problem as hepatitis. He had contracted it himself in Asia, and endured its effects on a long boat ride to Australia where the doctor told him simply to rest, eat a little toast, and wait for it to pass.

So I lay on my straw mattress in a tiny pension, feeling like death warmed up. I couldn't drink the polluted water, so I drank Pepsi twice a day. And I got weaker and weaker until finally I couldn't lift my hand from the mattress. I hit rock bottom. And then I started to get better and better, and within ten days of my arrival, I was riding on top of buses with the *campesinos* as they swung around river bends, clinging to narrow dirt roads between mountainside and riverbed, and starting to feel well enough to journey to Bogotá. I never did see the great pre-Columbian stone heads that were the most celebrated feature of the town, but I imbibed deeply the wild, febrile, natural forces of southern Colombia. And I had my first experience of long-term fasting, even if it was a Pepsi fast. This experience of illness and recovery taught me about the natural healing forces that lie within the body and the truth of Paracelsus' dictum that fasting is the awakener of the physician within.

Bogotá itself was the ill-lit, dangerous, crime-filled, highly eroticized city I had expected. Everywhere there were abandoned children sleeping in freezing doorways, stray dogs their only companions. Some were organized into bands of pickpockets in a truly Dickensian way. And everywhere there were green-uniformed police, called *aguacates*, and DAS, the corrupt, ubiquitous secret police who often shook down foreigners for whatever money they could get. The city was filled with small bars, inside of which there were scantily clad bar girls intent on persuading you to dance with them, buy them drinks, and more. The salsa and merengue, the miniskirts, the low-cut tops and bare midriffs, the flirtatious glances and pricey drinks, the constant erotic titillation of Bogotá were a big transition after months in the mountains and on the road.

The small Hotel Kaiser was near the city center and occupied by a number of bar girls with whom Paul and I soon developed a friendly connection. The difficulty of their lives was striking. Some had long-separated parents, fathers with nine children by eight separate women, and had been alone on the streets with just their wits and their bodies to help them survive since their early teens. I was struck by the traumas that everyone seemed to have experienced.

Colombia was intensely stressed and impoverished. *La Violencia*, the extremely violent and vicious civil war between Liberals and Conservatives, had terrorized millions into leaving their rural homes and heading to the city for safety and employment. Of course, there was not enough to be had — and countless men were forced into crime, women into bars, and children into doorways. It was like stepping back into the dark days of Victorian England with the added suffering of the 8,000-foot altitude and the icy, penetrating winds that blew across the *sabana* of Bogotá and froze the city at night.

Work wasn't easy to find. I did manage to make contact with a few businessmen whom I taught conversational English. I made in five to ten hours the equivalent of many working people's weekly wages. The city was filled with dark attractions and edgy experiences — women, drugs, risks, danger, and the ever-present vibe of violence and poverty.

I became close to a group of young, counterculture women living in Kennedy, the working-class district on the outskirts of Bogotá named after the American president. How bare their lives were. The brick houses and apartments were sparsely furnished; there were few educational opportunities, and virtually no jobs. Days consisted of hanging out with friends, strolling the barrio, thinking of little adventures, trying to get together a bit of money. One blessing was that the music scene in Bogotá was a few years behind the times and all the girls were obsessed with the Beatles and Rolling Stones; they would beg me to translate the song lyrics.

Everywhere in Colombia, the myth of *El Dorado*, the golden man, had left its residue. In every corner bar, desperately poor men were hatching schemes to make a million dollars. Colombians prided themselves on their street smarts, or *pilas*, their ability to read a situation quickly and find a way to take advantage of it. Petty crime was ubiquitous, and so, of course, were marijuana and cocaine. One day, one of the consummate street hustlers of our backstreet hotel showed me, with a grin, his collection of gold and emerald rings. He would wait outside the Hotel Tequendama — the main site for rich visitors to the city — then approach a tourist, offer his glamorously packaged wares while looking anxiously around for police, and then furtively offer a deal of a half or a third the marked cost, all while indicating that he was too nervous to stay and bargain. The tourists would snap up their deals, happy about their acumen, only to discover when they returned to their rooms that the rings were made of brass and the emeralds were chips of 7 Up bottles. He looked at me with a sly smile. "*¿Bonito no, hermano?*"

The dark milieu of the city was intensely exciting on the one hand, and deeply disturbing on the other. In the midst of it all, my spiritual search went on. In the early hours one morning, my roommates asleep, friends crashed on the floor, I had an inner experience that has remained with me my whole life. Listening to a record of Crosby, Stills & Nash singing, "Guinnevere had green eyes / Like yours, milady / Like yours," the awareness suddenly flooded me that I was here, on this earth, for one primary purpose — simply to be myself. I could make no greater contribution than to express my authentic nature in each moment as best I could. Living in this way was the path to both the greatest fulfillment and the greatest service. In the still silence of the night, I saw with total and unforgettable clarity that there was no better way for me to be than myself at all times. I realized I exist to be who I am, and that I do not have to pretend to be something I am not or someone whom others wish me to be. I am here to see what I see, feel what I feel, and speak what I know. From that point on, there could be no compromises. Personal authenticity and service to humanity came together. I could trust my inner self, that still voice within, and it would lead me along a path of integrity in the world. Such a simple insight, and yet so clear. That moment became a cornerstone of my journey through life.

As the weeks in Bogotá became months, the winter solstice began to approach. I still felt attuned to the cosmos, and the arrival of Comet Kohoutek seemed a significant fact. The heavens had arranged themselves so that this bright comet could be seen perfectly on December 23, when Bogotá would be one of the best places in the world to see a total eclipse of the sun. Cosmic occasions like this could certainly not be missed in the alternative spiritual ethos in which I was living. All those nights in the mountains of Bolivia and Peru taking in the vast, starlit skies had given me a sense of our place in the cosmos, our minuteness compared to the infinite space around us. Gazing in silence, night after night, at the endless galaxies and stars, it seemed indisputable that we are citizens of the cosmos. For us to imagine ourselves as separate would be like an atom in our fingernail imagining itself independent of our bodies. Such cosmic alienation could only have arisen in an industrialized culture cut off by artificial lights, stress, and television from the celestial panorama that offers itself each night. We skip our nocturnal reminder to be humble in the face of mystery at great peril. With the comet and the eclipse both approaching, there was a chance to reconnect strongly with the heavens.

News of this celestial synchronicity had spread far through the North American counterculture. Chuck, a longhaired, bearded, hippy Vietnam veteran with a love of the *I Ching* with whom I had formed a strong friendship in Ecuador, let me know he would be coming down from the San Francisco Bay Area with some Canadian friends for the big event. We decided to take a ramshackle local bus from the city high into the mountains above it. Our aim was to get off the dirt road in the middle of nowhere at the highest possible point and view the eclipse from there.

We found ourselves on a rough, grassy area high above a great valley that fell away below in almost sheer cliffs for thousands of feet. The wind was blowing strongly, and clouds and mist scurried across the sky forming a perfect filter through which we could view the eclipse. We wandered through patches of trees and shrubs looking for the perfect spot. Far below us, layers of cloud clung to the cliff sides like something from Conan Doyle's *The Lost World*.

We had just settled into a sheltered spot when we detected a growing rumble. A herd of bulls approached from a rough pasture nearby that we hadn't noticed. This was hardly what we had been looking forward to and we glared at them fiercely in a contest of bad vibes. They would stop and our attention would wander back to the imminent eclipse, but when we looked again they would have moved closer, as if ready to charge. It was turning into a manic switching between cosmic attunement and intense, earthly anxiety. As the cliff behind us fell away for thousands of feet, things were starting to shift from universal harmony to desperate flight, an ignominious retreat from celestial splendor to sheer survival.

One of my abiding memories of Colombia is the sight of Chuck, his poncho and long brown hair flying in the wind, running straight at the lead bull whirling his yellow-leather camera bag around his head and yelling fiercely. For a moment, the bulls edged forward, seemingly perplexed and angry. But as Chuck bore down on them, they hesitated, turned, and ran; the rest of us quickly headed for the nearest cover, exhaling a huge sigh of relief. Chuck had a rare bravery, an inherent fearlessness, and he endeared himself to us all for the remainder of his short life spent mostly on one sort of edge or another.

Now we could contemplate the heavens in peace. As the perfect orb of the moon began to slide across the face of the sun, half-darkness fell on the mountaintop and we gazed with wonder at the perfect symmetry of the cosmos. It was a sacred moment, a glimpse of transcendent harmony amidst the wilds and winds of this rough corner of the Andes. The trail of the comet could barely be distinguished in the semi-shade of the eclipse, but it was enough to strengthen that sense that comes from leaving cities and observing nature with reverence in remote places — the subtle sense of spiritual powers at work in the universe far greater in scope than we little humans. Later that afternoon, as we hiked among the bushes and hollows of this summit region, something in me awoke to the reality of the radiant essence as a power within my heart and within the heart of all people. In my heightened state, I felt myself letting go of lingering feelings of alienation and indifference to the spiritual path. A synthesis of rational mind and intuition came together, and I heard the word "initiation" throughout the day.

The deserts of the Southwestern United States had opened me up spiritually. I had been intrigued by Indian mystical philosophy, attracted to Sufism, drawn to the wisdom of the indigenous peoples of the Americas and their mysterious former civilizations. Now I found, totally unexpectedly, a new understanding of the sacred, and a greater sense of comfort with my own indigenous tradition. The name of that inner presence didn't matter. It was an experience of transcendent love at the heart of one's being, and a moment of spiritual self-realization that has stayed with me ever since.

A week later, I stood on the mountaintop of Monserrate, high above the city of Bogotá at the foot of the enormous statue of

Christ with arms extended in blessing that rivals the more famous one in Rio de Janeiro. It was predawn on New Year's morning, 1974 and I was twenty-four years old. The *sabana* or plain of Bogotá stretched out below, hidden by darkness. Above, the stars filled the serene night sky; below a great white cloud layer covered the city and stretched to the horizon.

At the moment of first light, a golden sunray shot out from the east and illuminated the sacred volcano of Tolima on the distant horizon. It was a moment of supreme harmony and order. The universe seemed to be unfolding as it should, the earth and the heavens circling in stately order. This was the vision of the cosmos that I had come looking for — above the madding crowd, on the mountaintop, attuned to the sacred features of the earthly landscape.

But as the morning progressed and the sun rose higher, its heat burned away the cloud layer below and revealed a seething, passionate city filled with suffering and injustice, with danger and confusion, just a few thousand feet below. This, I thought, speaks to my life's purpose. How do we bring that experience of calm, spiritual beauty, of an ordered cosmos guided by higher powers, into the frenzied rush and sweat and stress of big-city life? Can this mystical feeling of oneness with the universe be grounded in the darkness, the crime, the unhappiness of an urban environment created by intense materialism and a tragically unbalanced economic system? I didn't know it at the time, but these questions became a theme that would guide my path in the world for many years to come and show me a road to meaning and service.

Many months remained before I would finally depart this wild, beautiful, and tragic country. I saw one of my dearest Colombian woman friends rejected and demeaned by her Catholic family for an out-of-wedlock pregnancy; another friend, Tato the silversmith, was badly injured while trying to escape to North America. I even knew someone murdered for crossing a lover. Colombia was not a mellow place. Everyday life for so many poor people was filled with intense drama and suffering in abundance, and I could only have the greatest respect for their strength of character in the face of overwhelming obstacles that characterized the lives of so many poor Colombians.

By the time I left Colombia after almost a year there, I had developed a profound appreciation of human rights, the rule of law, and fundamentally honest government. In Bogotá, none of these things seemed to exist. If there was a legal problem, under-the-table payment to the judge and lawyer seemed the standard way of dealing with it.

When, in September 1974, my plane finally took off from Colombian territory and headed north towards California, I pumped my fist in the air with relief and joy that I had survived a year of intense, often dangerous existence in this country of extremes — beautiful, passionate, wounded women; sharp, quick, shrewd men in febrile cities; icy mountain plateaus and humid jungles. I thought of my Colombian friends in the working-class district of Kennedy who simply idled their days away without money or real hope of something different entering their lives. They were warm and gifted individuals, and I felt the narrowness of their existence and the suffocating economic limitations of so many in the "developing" world. It would only deepen my feeling for social justice and equality.

BERKELEY, CALIFORNIA, 1974

A few weeks after my arrival in the San Francisco Bay Area, I went to see a wise Chinese doctor. He was the kind of man who, through pulse and face diagnosis, could tell you how long you had been vegetarian. I still remember the short chuckle that he emitted as he registered my pulse, and the phrase that followed — "You carry on living like this, and you take ten years off your life."

Wise words indeed. I dutifully drank his foul-tasting herbal concoction twice every day, and my strength and calm began to return. I started to add a few healthy pounds to my skinny frame, and the balance of life began to be restored.

Enough stress, poverty, danger, indulgence, and anxiety in an unpredictable environment. I was back now in the land of consciousness, of sunshine, of the active, love-and-peace-based culture. Nixon was gone, the United States had withdrawn from Vietnam, the gardens and homes of Berkeley were bursting with beautiful flowers, temperatures were warm and mellow, everywhere there were people on the spiritual path, and for the first time in many months I could relax and beam *bonhomie* at those passing me on the street.

I was living now with my friend Chuck, his sister Jennifer, and my Canadian friends from South America, Simon and Ellen. We lived in the black neighborhood of Berkeley west of San Pablo Avenue surrounded by gently rundown houses and mostly friendly people. It was a period of nudity, freedom, fun, and wild spiritual exploration. California in 1974 was alive with countless groups concerned with the deeper mysteries of existence. In many ways, it was still the tail end of the '60s, and open sexuality, psychedelics, personal growth, Eastern religions, and Western esotericism all flourished in experimental form. After the harshness, violence, poverty, and cold of Bogotá, it felt like a sweet, sunny dream world of open people on the path to enlightenment. A trip to the Napa Valley would result in a stay at a small Sufi community among the vineyards where light-eyed artists were sketching their impressions of angelic presences among the grapes. A journey to Big Sur meant listening to the Pacific waves crash not far below, gazing at the star-filled skies, feeling the healing warmth relax body and soul, and pondering the experiments in consciousness that had already gone on for more than a decade with Aldous Huxley, Alan Watts, Abraham Maslow, Fritz Perls, and many others.

Just the name Aldous Huxley was enough to evoke for me elements of the Perennial philosophy, the universal stream of wisdom that flowed through every culture and that had been marginalized in our overly rational and materialistic West. Not everyone understood that Huxley, aided by his encounter with psychedelics, had moved far beyond the dystopia of the Brave New World for which he was so well known to a profoundly spiritual worldview. I thought of him as someone who had escaped the grayness of Britain that so oppressed my teenage soul. His experiments with mescaline had opened his scholarly mind to realms of philosophy too long neglected by the academic and cultural establishment. He seemed a pioneer, a forerunner of the shift from a drab, black-and-white world of small philosophical ideas to a colorful, spiritually expansive experience of the universe.

It was now the waning months of the Vietnam War and things were going very badly from the perspective of the American government. President Ford seemed immobilized, overwhelmed by forces beyond his control. But the Berkeley counterculture felt vindicated with the war now revealed as the catastrophe in the making that wiser heads had long predicted. So despite the economic problems and the dire international situation, there was a sense of jubilation, expansion, and freedom in the air.

In Berkeley itself, hundreds of groups and initiatives devoted to penetrating the truth of spiritual and psychological reality flourished. The first group of alternative healers I met in the Bay Area was the Church of the Gentle Brothers and Sisters, gay and lesbian healers who used palm reading to diagnose a person's physical, psychological, and spiritual problems, and treated them with circles of magnificent, resounding, lengthy Oms. The person needing healing lay on a table and the Brothers and Sisters surrounded him, holding hands, and began a cascade of rising and falling, harmonic, sacred Sanskrit sounds that was sustained for five or ten minutes while the person on the receiving end soaked up the heart-centered attention, the good vibrations, and the beautiful cadences of the Church members. These multiple-toned, resonant Oms seemed to balance the subtle bodies of the person on the receiving end, who absorbed the beautiful cadences. Occult and New Age bookstores proliferated, perfumed by Indian incense and filled with the works of the older generations of spiritual writers — Madame Blavatsky, Max Heindel, Manly P. Hall, and Dion Fortune from the West; and Swami Vivekananda, Ramakrishna, and Yogananda from the East. These volumes sat side by side with the works of Ram Dass, Timothy Leary, and the post-psychedelic thinkers who tried to ground the flashes of cosmic insight into intelligible prose.

But for me, there was one writer who spoke above all others at this point in my life. During my year in Colombia, I had read a short pamphlet by Dane Rudhyar, the French-born composer, philosopher, and astrologer that had brought clarity and meaning to my own life situation. He had emigrated from France before the First World War and avoided the fate of his peers in his home village, all of whom are said to have died on the battle-front. Arriving in America as a young man, he was part of that early wave of esoteric thinkers and artists whose work preceded the consciousness explosion of the '60s by four decades. He had an ability to construct sentences that brought to perfect, elegant expression various thoughts and insights that had floated around my own mind for years in incoherent form. It sometimes seemed that his words conveyed insights that my own higher self had been trying to get through to me. He had a grandeur of vision and a level of spiritual awareness that nourished my soul as I was integrating the wild, often dangerous experiences of South America.

Ever since my first encounter with his writings, I had felt a resonance with his phrases, often finding perfectly expressed original thoughts that resounded like a lingering bell tone in my psyche. No other writer seemed to encapsulate my growing spiritual awareness so perfectly, so trenchantly, so nobly.

Years later, when I finally had the chance to spend time with him in his modest home in Palo Alto, I found him humble, wise, and attentive with his owlish but charming demeanor and still-thick French accent.

I had resolved while still in Colombia that if I ever made it out of there in one piece, I would have Dane Rudhyar to thank in significant measure. Chuck had brought down a small pamphlet of his to Bogotá that was filled with wisdom and insight. He was a Renaissance man steeped in music, psychology, and philosophy. On reaching California, I had been especially taken with his book *We Can Begin Again Together: A Reevaluation of the Basic Concepts of Western Civilization*. He wasn't a man for small tasks. "Beaten paths are for beaten men," was one of his maxims.

I sent him a small donation and thanked him for his gift of wisdom that had been so helpful in dark times. He responded by putting me in touch with a circle of people in Berkeley seeking star wisdom. They met in a small cabin in a back garden. My first night one friendly and engaging man told of monitoring an astronomy class at the University of California, Berkeley where he had just learned that some of the remotest specks of light at the edge of the known universe were not just stars, nor were they merely solar systems, nor even galaxies. They were galaxies of galaxies. After all the nights in the Andes gazing at the star-filled sky, this astronomical insight sank deeply into my sense of reality.

This circle of admirers of Dane Rudhyar introduced me to special friends, with whom I stayed close for the year I spent on the West Coast. I happily count Dane Rudhyar among the wise beings who helped me find coherence and meaning in life. From him I gained a sense of the overarching harmony of the cosmos, and the mysterious, esoteric underpinnings of life and destiny. For that, I will always be grateful.

The open eroticism of the West Coast counterculture also appealed to me strongly. I returned home one day to find forty naked people massaging each other on the floor of the living room. A friend had to leave, and I was invited to take his place massaging a young woman to whom I was definitely attracted and who seemed to reciprocate. Another friend worked part time as a porn star. She could make a thousand dollars a day back in an era when few women were willing to do it, and most of those who did were counterculture "freaks." She thought nothing of wandering into the living room naked and sitting down for breakfast with three clothed men, resplendent in her large, brown nipples and sexy grin.

I was loving this. It seemed like a golden time to me after the harshness of Colombia. The constant California sunshine; the scents of eucalyptus and pine on Mount Tamalpais; the soothing presence of water everywhere in the Bay Area; the culture bursting with people engaged in quests and personal growth. All these things happily soothed my soul after the tests of South America.

There was a person who particularly intrigued me: Oscar Ichazo. As I had returned from nearly two years in Latin America, I was very interested in the son of a Bolivian general who was said to have learned from the shamans on his father's Andean estates, studied with kabbalists in Buenos Aires, journeyed to China and Tibet in search of alchemical and tantric secrets, and drunk deeply from the well of Sufi wisdom. Not only that, he had produced a scientific approach to the training of consciousness that offered a guaranteed path to enlightenment, and a very attractive blend of mind and body with its mix of martial arts, psycho-calisthenics, and emotional karma cleaning. In those days, it was a question of discerning between the genuine and the fake in the spiritual bazaar that alternative California had become. Usually, there was no way to find out without exploring in person, and having fun trying.

So when I had the chance to attend a forty-day Arica training in the Rocky Mountain National Park in Estes Park, Colorado, I jumped at it. I needed a period of sustained body / mind discipline and intense focus on the development of consciousness. I wasn't attracted to the more traditional worlds of yoga and Buddhist meditation. I was looking for something new and fresh. The pure mountain air, the grandeur of the Rockies, and the endless snowy expanses were just what my soul needed. I loved the training and its mix of physical workouts, psychological clearing, and spiritual practices from many traditions. My goal was to find a way to replicate through disciplined practice the states of spiritual openness and inspiration that I had experienced on mountaintops, at sacred sites like Machu Picchu, and on the shores of Lake Titicaca.

And indeed, it proved a deeply valuable experience that restored me to full wellness. The morning psycho-calisthenics proved a strong workout after the indulgences of South America. The karma cleaning, as the process of self-revelation was called, was exacting, and I greatly appreciated the heightened vitality, the bonds of connection, and the use of practices from a wide range of esoteric cultures. By the end of the forty days, I was bursting with vitality, brimming with positivity, feeling in the best physical and mental shape in years, and running around the snow-covered Rockies with exuberant zest.

Perhaps I would take Arica to the next level and go to New York for the advanced training. Meanwhile, California still beckoned. In those days, I felt so much freedom. Ever since my study of existentialism at university in Sussex, I had loved the sheer exercise of my existential freedom to do and be as I chose. Now I would return West, but the feeling was rising up in me that it was time to make a contribution to society.

I had traveled widely and gained much since I had first decided to leave graduate school and devote myself fulltime to the exploration of deeper forms of reality. Now the feeling arose with increasing frequency that I wanted to find a place to apply my energies. It was time to create something that expressed my deepest values and insights. I no longer doubted the legitimacy of the spiritual worldview. It was clear to me that powerful, unconscious forces guided the psyche, and that life was infinitely more complex, mysterious, and meaningful than our culture was currently able to acknowledge.

One weekend back on the West Coast, my friends and I decided to visit the Napa Valley, the wine-growing mecca of Northern California. We were staying at a small Sufi community surrounded by vineyards when I picked up a book by English writer John Michell explicating the connections between mysterious "ley lines" (the old, straight tracks that seemed to cover large parts of Britain and link up the churches of St. Michael and St. George), old stone circles, ancient crossroads, and forgotten notches on the horizon, weaving into one gigantic and elusive symmetry.

I also came across a small green pamphlet called "Findhorn: A Center of Light" by Paul Hawken. It told the story of a community in northern Scotland whose spiritual practice was attunement to nature and whose goal was to build a center of demonstration, a place that showed that a new, ecologically aware, spiritually awake world could be built with courage, perseverance, persistence, and inner guidance.

I resolved that when next I returned to my country of origin, I would walk those ley lines and travel up to Moray in northern

Scotland. I was starting to feel that back in the land of my birth, far from the exotic climes of the Western Hemisphere, similar mysteries to those of the pre-Columbian cultures of the Maya and Inca might be found. Perhaps I could return to Britain with eyes made new and find the missing spiritual element, the absence of which had made me so eager to leave years before.

I had begun to feel that the period of emphasis on my spiritual search was coming to a close, and that it was time to serve humanity in some way. I wanted a consciousness skill. I wanted to support the awakening of others while working on my own inner development. And I liked the mysticism of Arica, its multicultural influences, and its attention to both mind and body.

So I said a poignant farewell to Carol, my sweet and artistically talented girlfriend in Berkeley, the woman with whom I'd connected at the massage party, and joined a bunch of crazy guys driving pretty much nonstop to the Big Apple in a battered old green car with a huge engine, no radio, and no heat. I arranged through my friend, the porn actress who was a New Yorker by origin, for a few places to crash in the city, and headed East. It was a touching goodbye to California with its friendships, its gorgeous natural beauty, its vibrant consciousness movement, its free and open sexuality, and its physical comfort and safety.

When the skyscrapers and urban density of New York finally came into sight, and the tenements began to appear, cramped and dirty, I started to feel strongly the suffering and anguish of millions of lonely immigrants in their struggle to adapt to a new, harsh, frightening world. When my co-drivers dropped me off on Manhattan's East Side, Wayne, our short-order cook and car owner, remarked with his offbeat mix of humor and cynicism that I looked like I fit right in. Little did he or I know how right he was.

It was hot, sticky, and sweaty in New York in the summer of 1975 as I made my way to the Arica headquarters. I was charmed by the *yantras* on the walls, mystical symbols the contemplation of which was said to strengthen the awakening of consciousness. But I was perplexed by the older students walking around in meditation suits whose colors indicated the level of training they had completed. There was talk of creating a twentieth-century mystery school in the city, but I felt uneasy about the gradations that were creeping into the student body.

In the ancient world, it may have been helpful or even necessary to distinguish outwardly between different kinds of initiates in the mystery centers. In 1975 it seemed to me there was the danger of confusing those who simply had the money to complete various higher levels of training with those who genuinely had achieved more enlightened states of consciousness.

There was no question that there was something brilliant in the forty-day training and its unique mix of disciplines. I had no objection to those who wished to follow this path, but I saw clearly that it wasn't for me.

Now what to do? With my meager funds down to a few hundred dollars, should I go to Canada? Should I return to Britain? One fetid night in lower Manhattan, I tracked down the Broome Street Bar in SoHo that had been recommended to me at my last party in Marin County before my departure from California. As I entered the small space between the inner and outer doors, my gaze fell on a notice board covered in small paper signs and announcements. I turned to my companion and remarked, "Maybe I'll find a cheap flight here." Literally at the end of my forefinger was a note saying CHEAP FLIGHTS TO LONDON.

How should I read this sign? Once again, my life hung in the balance. Whether to go north, west, or east — that was the question. I had just enough to buy the ticket, and remembering my interest in the remote Scottish community and the strange world of ley lines and stone circles, I decided to go for it. I had not seen my family in Yorkshire in three-and-a-half years. After countless experiences on my quest for meaning, I wanted to put down some roots — to find a place to give back to the world.

The stone of fate was tossed into the center of the pond. How would its ripples touch my life and its purpose? A few days later, I showed up at Kennedy Airport and stepped onto the plane. *Hasta luego*, las Americas. Britain beckoned with all its history, its old-fashioned esotericism, its neolithic mysteries, and its family ties. A rich chapter of my life closed, and the time approached when I would see if my intense spiritual convictions, my burning sense of the need to create a new culture, could be grounded in the soil of my native land.

PART TWO

THE WORK

CHAPTER SIX

∞

FINDHORN, NORTHERN SCOTLAND

THE HEART EXPANDS, THE SOUL FINDS COMMUNITY

New Year's Eve, 1975. In the snowy darkness, my train pulled up at Forres Station in the north of Scotland, and I stepped onto the platform in this remote world far from the warmth of California. My old friend Simon, veteran of Colombia and the Andes, was there to greet me. He and his wife Ellen had visited this spiritual community based on an attunement to and love of nature, and had sent back glowing reports.

We drove along winding country lanes toward the small village of Findhorn, passing a strange, ancient standing stone by the side of the road, and in the biting wind pulled up in front of a low building known as the community center where dinner was being served. I walked inside and took off my coat. A pair of swinging doors blocked my view of the interior where it appeared, from the buzz of good humor, that most of the community members were present. I walked toward them and entered the dining room. Immediately I experienced a feeling that warmed my heart and that I still remember vividly almost forty years later — "But I know half these people!" I had never lain eyes on nearly all of them before but my sense of comfort and familiarity was instantaneous.

Thus began a saga that in one sense lasted three-and-a-half years in northern Scotland, but that in other ways was to go on for twenty-five years, as I worked to create and maintain "centers of light" in Findhorn language, or places where a new consciousness could emerge. On that snowy Scottish night in the mid-'70s I could never have guessed that my path would take me from this distant Northern outpost on the edge of the Moray Firth to the heart of downtown Manhattan via the hills and valleys of upstate New York.

Findhorn in the mid-1970s was a very special place. Entering the community, it was as if you passed through a semi-palpable wall of love into a realm possessing some of the charm and beauty of Tolkien's Rivendell. It had all begun in 1962 when Peter and Eileen Caddy and their Canadian friend Dorothy Maclean found themselves out of work and money, living on a caravan site. They had been pioneers in the postwar British spiritual movement. Eileen and Dorothy had developed remarkable meditative powers, and Peter translated into action the inner guidance received from the two women. What came to them in contemplation was that this unlikely caravan park was to become a world-famous community to which people would come to create a center of light, demonstrating that it is possible to live together largely harmoniously in a state of loving attunement to nature.

It must have taken remarkable faith to believe that any of this could possibly come true before the psychedelic era and the Beatles had opened up a widespread interest in meditation and spirituality. Yet when I arrived thirteen years after that first beginning the place was thriving and hopping. Ever since David Spangler, a young and brilliantly gifted American spiritual teacher and writer, had come to Findhorn at the beginning of the '70s, the place had been transformed from what must have appeared to outsiders as a small group of a dozen or so aging English eccentrics into a vibrant international community filled with energetic, young people bursting with idealism and dedication to a new spiritual vision. This was the group that greeted me as I crossed the threshold to the community center on that snowy New Year's Eve. They were from all over the world but the largest contingent, apart from the Brits, was American, and they exuded that fine American quality: "can do."

Morayshire, where Findhorn is located, has an open, picturesque beauty about it. What it lacks in the craggy wildness that characterizes the western coast of Scotland, it makes up for in forests, fields, hills, and ancient monuments. "The land of witches and warlocks," according to compilations of mythological Scotland, where Macbeth meets the witches who say, "Double, double, toil and trouble."

An old Victorian hotel and hydro spa, Cluny Hill, five miles away in the ancient town of Forres, had just been purchased for a mere 60,000 pounds to accommodate the increasing number of visitors showing up from every corner of the planet. This would be my home for most of my time at Findhorn.

I would wake each morning at Cluny to the sweet cooing of wood pigeons. From the front of the old hotel, the forested land rose gradually toward the southern horizon. A pale dawn light, seen often in the winter months when the sun rose as late as 10 AM, filled the sky with a soothing presence. Behind the Victorian pile, the hill climbed steeply to the "power point," a spot thought to be a significant site for subtle earth energies, and certainly a place of beauty and mystery.

Five miles away, the caravan park where the Findhorn Community came into existence lay quietly by the bay. Beyond the sand dunes, the breakers of the Moray Firth crashed steadily along the pebbly beach. Nimrod jets from RAF Kinloss, fresh from hunting Soviet submarines, often shattered the silence as they came in to land less than half a mile from the flimsy trailers and simple bungalows that made up the community.

A pentagonal Universal Hall was being constructed on the edge of the sand dunes just past the studio where Findhorn printed and bound its deep but simple messages of love and harmony. Designed according to principles of sacred geometry, it was a wildly ambitious project. Like everything in the community, it was started with little or no money — just an abundance of faith that this was in harmony with the spiritual purpose of this center of light, and that support would come. And indeed it did.

White-haired granddads jubilantly passed cinderblocks down long lines of workers as the Hall gradually rose from the sand. The occasional opera-loving Italian American filled the fresh, clear air with songs of simple happiness as the line sustained its pace. There were solstice meditations with 400 people in the still-unfinished shell of the Hall when utter silence descended and the group felt blessed as if sublimely embraced by the wings of a great angel. There is nothing to rival the pure silence of hundreds of people in meditation, and there were times when it seemed that a great ensouling presence was ever so slightly discernible in the Hall, an extra quality of stillness, depth, and peace.

The '70s were a time of inspiration during which the vitality of a generation inspired by Woodstock was poured into spiritual endeavors instead of war and moneymaking. Back then we were intent on transforming the world for the better, making it a more spiritually conscious place, opening people up to the natural love deep within each of them, and cultivating our appreciation of the mysterious forces that create the beauties of nature around us. I had no attraction to any center that focused on gurus or some tightly prescribed spiritual path, but I was drawn to Findhorn as its emphasis was practical and non-dogmatic — let's build the new together, and have fun doing it.

Through my journeys across the deserts of the American Southwest, down the Pan-American Highway to Peru and Bolivia, and deep in the snow-covered Rockies, I had sought a spiritual vision that would give meaning to my life. I had experienced moments of insight, expanded awareness, and a deep sense that the contemporary world needed spiritual transformation, beginning with the West. This rebirth needed to run parallel with political, social, and environmental change to have enduring benefit. As I reached my mid-twenties, the question had become one of where to begin. Now in the north of Scotland, back on the island of my birth after so many distant wanderings, I had somewhere to start.

I have always enjoyed initiating things, and when I heard of this new branch of Findhorn at Cluny Hill, I knew it was the place for me. Besides, I had no money to stay in the community, and those crazy enough to volunteer for that first summer at Cluny were asked to contribute nothing financially. It wasn't hard to see why. When the enormous, rundown old building had been purchased a few months earlier, the previous owners were already contracted to accept coach parties of pensioners and tourists making a stop on their tour of the Highlands. This was how the hotel had paid for itself for decades and there was no way to wriggle out of the deal.

So when the spring of 1976 arrived, after months of desperate work cleaning the grotesquely dirty old kitchen and the blood-congealed pantry, attempting to fix the radiators, staying up all night laying linoleum in the kitchen corridor listening to the Beach Boys, the first coach party arrived. It was a strange transition. One moment we were citizens of the New Age; the next minute we were carrying guests' bags up to their rooms and accepting tips for our efforts. The first to arrive was a group of old-age pensioners from England, and it rained the whole week they were there. But from the moment they arrived and were greeted by the whole staff waving greetings, they loved it. At the end, they told us that we had revived their faith in human nature.

That original group of Cluny Loonies, as we termed ourselves, worked the summer of the coach parties and came from all over the world: Hawaii, Zimbabwe, Vancouver, New York, Amsterdam, Glasgow, Perthshire, Boston and the Midwest, California and Southern England. Somehow we were all drawn to this mad task of renovating a hopelessly neglected old Highland hotel and turning it into a center of light. When we painted the dark and grimy basement, we visualized light in each white paint stroke. From cooking breakfast to cleaning floors, we tried to put consciousness into all we did. It was the only time in my life when I fell asleep the instant my head hit the pillow, so intense and exhausting was our effort. And it was all accomplished with enormous good humor, warmth, and laughter fueling our dedication. There have been other moments in my life when I have experienced a comparable fellowship to the one we knew — but they have been rare. I will feel a bond with most of those characters until my dying day, and whenever I see them, I am always filled with affection.

Cluny had been acquired to enable Findhorn to accommodate its growing visitors, so once the coach-party summer was over, dealing with the guest groups became a central feature of our lives. It was here that I first learned about group dynamics. Findhorn's international fame as a place of contemporary spiritual inspiration was growing dramatically, thanks to the pamphlet by Paul Hawken that I had read in California and to international tours by the founders in which Peter's natural showmanship moved and inspired thousands.

Each week groups and individuals would arrive from every corner of the planet with participants from a broad social and national spectrum — German businessmen, Australian hippies, Californian housewives from Santa Monica, grannies from the

English Midlands, retired generals from the U.S. military, and so on. The mix of each week was unique and outrageous. And yet in the vast majority of instances, by the time we were three days into the program, the reserve and sense of distance and separation between people had gone, and an amazing process of unification and love was occurring. The groups would work in the kitchen, garden, and do housekeeping or maintenance for half the day, and do group activities the other half — simple "group discovery" exercises that encouraged openness, readings from David Spangler's works of spiritual insight, and trips to places of natural beauty on the River Findhorn in the moist, silent forest. There was no cunningly designed process to induce people to change. The simple aura of loving warmth and connection between people in those days, allied with the sense of dedication to the larger mission of creating a center of demonstration, was enough to make people glow.

At the end of each week, when the group members described their experiences, the change was usually phenomenal. Simply place people into an atmosphere as conducive to love as Findhorn was, and they blossomed. Hearts opened, fears fell away, laughter flowed. In my whole life I do not believe I ever had as much fun in a group context. These were days of innocence and hope in which all the dedicated idealism of youth permeated everything we did.

At Findhorn before any meal, meeting, or work session there was always a moment of silent attunement during which we all held hands in a circle. But the place was never sanctimonious. The members were not weak characters looking desperately for some guru or guide. Instead, they were strong, independent, gifted people who chose to come together behind a common purpose that spoke to the deepest feelings in their hearts. And there was plenty of comedy and parody of the New Age life, and lots of poking fun at Peter and Eileen and other authority figures at the community sharings held every Friday night. When a wonderful old German dance master, Bernard Wosien, arrived and taught us the beauties of European sacred folk dance, a generation of rock and rollers morphed into a dance troupe and performed sacred myths set to music and movement.

Of course, life wasn't perfect, and the same melodramas of love and relationship that characterized ordinary existence were as present at Findhorn as anywhere else. But there was a huge reservoir of goodwill, good humor, and simple love that flowed in all directions. After my years of travel and adventure in South America, the mean streets of Chicago, and elsewhere, this was a place for my own healing. True, it wasn't exactly intellectual, but that was not due to any lack of intelligence among the members. It was the result of emphasis on development of the heart and intuition, which, in turn, created the aura of love that warmed us all when we came in from the cold of a spiritually lost society.

So many of us were products of an education that had neglected the heart, soul, and imagination. My own spiritual journey had shown me many times that the essence of living was love, and that we needed to create a society in which love predominated over its countless rivals. So in northern Scotland in the mid-'70s, we weren't looking for abstract or postmodern theories. We wanted a vivid experience of loving community and an environment of natural beauty in which to practice the opening of the heart and the stilling of the mind.

People came from all over the world to Findhorn because in the '70s there simply were not many places like it. You had Esalen in California's Big Sur, but that was a place that emphasized psychology and bodywork rather than the creation of a spiritual community. There was Auroville in India, inspired by the work of Sri Aurobindo, but it was inaccessible to most Westerners. Findhorn took effort to reach — at the very least long train rides from London — but it had the merit of being in Europe and connected to the Western spiritual stream. It also had tales of magic, of encounters with beings from the invisible world, and of almost miraculous coincidences that had enabled this spiritual center to survive and thrive with almost no formal support from the outside world. Peter had meticulously followed Eileen's inner guidance and Dorothy's attunement to the messages of the *devas*, or angelic beings who stood behind the world of nature. Furthermore, R. Ogilvie Crombie, a wise, elderly Scottish esotericist, had encountered nature spirits and even the great being, Pan, in places as distinct as the Edinburgh botanical gardens and St. Columba's cell on the isle of Iona, and had brought his insights to the community. Then came David Spangler with his intuitive contact with higher worlds and his articulate, heart-centered wisdom.

People began to show up convinced that they had been guided by higher powers to live at Findhorn — despite the fact that, in some cases, nobody knew they were coming, they were penniless, and often there was no accommodation for them. I well remember the time a couple and their three children arrived at the community from Hawaii with zero warning, convinced that the spiritual world had given them instructions to do so. It was a time and a place where the hand of the divine was intuited in many things, when people lived with a strong sense that we are all divine beings of great potential, when higher worlds wished us well and supported us in our spiritual development towards self-realization. This gave a marvelous élan to the place and enabled the members to live in a state of joy when they were not caught in their own personal tribulations. We felt that we were working in harmony with the needs of both this world and the higher world, and things were working out wonderfully well. Peter was filled with stories of how bales of hay had happened to fall off a truck just when the community needed compost, of how this person with that particular skill had shown up or "manifested" at just the right moment when he was needed for some fresh project, or how some donation had come along at just the right time. He was a man of remarkable faith that was inspiring in its optimism, and life seemed to be working out in our favor as we devoted our youthful energies to a high and noble endeavor recognized and aided by the spiritual worlds.

We had people of all generations as members. As someone who had imagined that anybody who chose to make a career of the military was dumb or daft, I was amazed to meet the gracious and ever-cheerful Ross Stewart, the chairman of the board of trustees, who had captained a battle cruiser in the Second World War. Before Findhorn, I had never spent time with anyone who had chosen the military as a serious profession. My father had seen a lot of death in the Second World War, and had always been clear that war was horrific and devoid of glamour. At Findhorn, I came to know and respect a former British army colonel and major, RAF lieutenants and squadron leaders, and the occasional navy commander. These were clearly men of integrity, sensitivity, and goodwill. There were qualities of decency, cheerfulness, and humility that, while not universal among Findhorn's former military officers, did emanate from the majority of them. Perhaps it was the warrior spirit that seems to quietly permeate the atmosphere of Highland Scotland, but I came to see how essentially noble human beings might choose the military path as a form of service to humanity.

There was also a strong contingent of elderly ladies, mostly English, who got along famously with the young American post-hippies. Although the community at that time was almost totally white, it crossed all age ranges and had a booming baby population.

In the mid-'70s the spirit at Findhorn was wonderful, and the morale could not have been higher. Paul Hawken's book, *The Magic of Findhorn*, was just out, attracting people in droves to the community. Who knew what remarkable and brilliant beings might alight from the bus each Saturday morning at Cluny Hill to begin a new guest week? Which of them would stay and add their talents to the membership? The community was also expanding dramatically. First the 150-bed Cluny Hill, then Drumduan House overlooking Findhorn Bay, then Station House in Findhorn Village, and other properties donated or bought. Everything seemed on a roll.

But there were challenges in the community emerging that related, unsurprisingly, to the awareness of higher spiritual worlds. How does a group of people remain firmly grounded and sensible when the existence of nature spirits, angels, and guiding spiritual intelligences are woven into the foundation of its worldview? Initially, Eileen Caddy had received guidance for Peter and the small community of the '60s in her nightly meditations. She was a woman who, beneath the guise of a middle-class English matron, was a person of deep simplicity and integrity who had developed over many years an attunement to her inner voice. Her "still, small voice" was possessed of genuine wisdom and was a huge source of inspiration in the early years. But as the initial group of members grew into an international community, her inner sense directed her to stop giving guidance to the community. And not long afterward, her inner sense instructed her to conclude the private guidance for Peter himself.

It was time for the community to figure out for itself its own decisions and directions in an entirely self-responsible way. This must have been very difficult for Peter. As someone who was the first to admit he had no contemplative capacities, seeing himself instead as a man of action, he was suddenly bereft of contact with the spiritual world that had inspired him since youth. David Spangler's intelligent and gentle presence filled this gap until 1973, but with his departure Peter was suddenly without a figure whose wisdom and insight could be trusted without question.

This left an unfortunate residue of susceptibility to individuals claiming contact with higher worlds as Peter had an understandable desire to feel he was doing work attuned to the highest possible needs. There was no shortage of psychics, intuitives, sensitives — or whatever term we gave them — who were more than willing to bend the ear of one of the founders of this increasingly famous community. In his wife, and in their founding colleague Dorothy Maclean, he had enjoyed the insights of two women of genuine depth and spiritual alignment. Now he was exposed to the spiritual supermarket of those claiming inner contact with higher beings — with mixed results.

For me this was a big lesson in the dangers of overdependence on others to provide spiritual insight and guidance. Access to intuitive wisdom through others can become an addiction that is very hard to break. Far better to develop a contemplative practice for oneself, even if it never approaches the clarity of one's original mentors. But this was not Peter's path, and he became perhaps overly susceptible to those able to present themselves as exceptionally attuned to "the divine plan."

This was his weak point — and, of course, we all have them. But aside from this, he was a remarkable leader in many ways. Peter's conviction that he was doing the work of higher worlds gave him the gift of instilling in others a sense of the urgent importance of any task at hand. Everything took on the heightened intensity of a military mission, even if it was just a drive to Iona to pick up some members leaving the island or the need to finish part of the Universal Hall before a conference began. He was always all over the community in his tweed jacket with his bald pate and erect bearing. He was a man of huge energy, positivity, discipline, and focus who bridged the gap between the old world of prewar British esotericism and the post-'60s world of eclectic spirituality. Eileen's quiet contemplative mode and Peter's vigorous inspiration together produced a brew of rare potency on the many tours across America, Europe, and Australia that they conducted in the '70s, telling people everywhere of this unique community in this unlikely location.

Findhorn always saw itself as part of an emerging planetary "network of light," or collection of centers devoted to what the twenty-first century would call spirituality, ecology, and sustainability. These centers, it was felt, had the capacity to become hubs from which new values and practices could emanate and gradually transform human consciousness. And in the '70s they began popping up everywhere, sometimes inspired by Findhorn's example. Down in Tennessee, the former Marine and San Francisco State College teacher Stephen Gaskin had founded the Farm at the end of a long journey 'round America in a convoy of old school buses. At its peak, over a thousand people lived there growing soybeans, exploring tantric sex, and using marijuana as a sacrament. There was the new Renaissance community in Turners Falls, Massachusetts, where the church choir was an all-girl rock and roll group, and community members rode into town on Sunday morning on their Harley-Davidsons, departing their 2001 Center in the countryside for a spiritual service at the renovated old opera house. There was the Abode of the Message, an upstate New York Sufi community that birthed the Omega Institute.

A lot of the hippies who'd gone back to the land in the '60s abandoned their efforts when times became too rough. But some survived and prospered, and these initiatives often provided the seeds from which more enduring communities would sprout. Today there are thousands of places all over the developed world — spas, retreat centers, urban learning centers — that embody a holistic approach to life. Perhaps their influence has been modest compared to the immense tide of greed and materialism that has gripped Western culture in the '80s, '90s, and beyond. But they continue their work quietly and, when the obsession with loads of money, SUVs, and the glories of the stock market fades, they will be there offering succor to those needing something deeper and more authentic.

In the '70s, it was wonderful to feel yourself part of an emerging planetary culture. The magic of Findhorn involved a lot more than the encounters of unusually sensitive and aware people with beings from beyond the sense-perceptible world. It was the marvelous joy and companionship that comes from working together on the creation of a noble vision. It was learning to see beyond people's outer form — their age, class, or nationality — to see their inner beauty. It was about seeing the power of combined focused intention among a group of people well attuned to each other whether it was renovating a building, preparing a vegetarian banquet, or moving large rocks along a human chain from beach to truck.

In my own life, it was a time of innocence and beauty. I was not innocent about the world. No one who has spent a year of their youth in the poor quarters of Bogotá, Colombia can claim much innocence still intact. But I was still relatively innocent of the shadow within spiritual undertakings — the role of ego in people who feel that their commitment to deeper values has taken them beyond concern with such ignoble matters. It is a sad truth that many people whose primary sense of identity is that of a spiritual person consider themselves incapable of being politically manipulative, and thus become dangerously unconscious of their own shadows. The experience of Findhorn for me was overwhelmingly positive, but it left a residue of concern about the political and psychological naïveté of goodhearted individuals who see themselves exclusively as beings of love and light devoid of the dark instincts that create sadness in this profane world.

My own story in the community was relatively simple. In the spring of 1976, I was appointed to focalize the maintenance department of this huge nineteenth-century building. The large crew from Findhorn had finished their work of renovation over the winter, and we were now preparing for the coach parties. Unfortunately, I knew absolutely nothing about maintenance. Changing a light bulb and unplugging a drain with a stick were about my only abilities in this field. And I was now responsible for every radiator, toilet, doorjamb, and stuck window in the place, not to mention the regular checking of the new boilers. My only colleague at this point, Stan, was an equally unskilled Californian whose primary responsibility was to be night porter. We still recall our comic misadventures balancing on top of ladders trying to free the drains from clogging by autumn leaves. I was pretty ignorant when it came to maintenance, but when Stan suggested on our first day at work that since Scots drove on the left, we should screw things into the wall by turning the screwdriver to the left, I felt downright knowledgeable — though wildly out of my depth.

Thankfully, the rumors of a mysterious trio on their way to Cluny Hill from Hawaii making slow but steady progress driving across the United States turned out to be true. Edward was a maintenance expert — a professional pipefitter, no less. He taught me everything I know about hanging doors, laying linoleum, performing basic carpentry, and, of course, changing pipes. It was notable how many American and Australian former hippies had a broad range of construction and building skills. They all seemed to know how to fix cars and roof buildings and pour concrete, and eventually my own finest hour came when I built a garbage fence at the back of the Cluny Hill bar. It was greatly to Peter Caddy's credit that he never subscribed to a notion of an alcohol-free community. His years in the catering branch of the RAF during World War II, when he had been responsible for feeding men along a great stretch of the Burma front, had shown him the morale-building value of a drink with dinner, and he never exercised sanctimoniousness.

After a long summer spent in maintenance and as a bus driver, navigating RAF surplus buses with primitive gearboxes around small, winding Scottish roads, I wound up joining the guest department. It was usual at Findhorn for people to be placed in areas in which they had no expertise so they did not bring egotistical notions of their own superiority to the task at hand. I quickly learned to enjoy the work with guest groups and the amazing outpouring of love that came from almost all of them. It was as if the true nature of each individual, the innermost radiant and pure heart, had emerged from slumber and was emanating joy and appreciation. I recall great bursts of laughter, tales of hearts broken, and healed, spiritual paths lost and found, and unexpected delights in the details of everyday life like washing dishes and weeding gardens. But there was also often an element of fear — fear of returning to the dark, cold world outside where it would be so much harder to maintain and express the inner light.

We learned that it was very difficult to retain the Findhorn glow long after departure. The average person found themselves removed abruptly from this enchanted realm where life was deeply meaningful, where normal, sane people experienced higher worlds, and where hundreds labored to create a new, more love-infused way of living. Suddenly they were back in that dreary, material world of factories, malls, and all the sad, soul-wearying detritus of consumer capitalism. I, myself, was always glad to get back to Findhorn, even from the small town of Forres nearby. I was happy to be with people on the same path as myself, joining their energies to build something hopeful and beautiful instead of the grim grind of jobs, money, and mortgages into which so many formerly free spirits had been unwittingly sucked.

When the time came to leave toward the end of the '70s, it was a bittersweet moment. The world at large was drawing me strongly, but I looked back on many fond memories: the collective focus, warmth, and laughter of the Cluny Hill kitchen crew that enabled me to produce a rhubarb crumble for a hundred diners on my first attempt at dessert; the contemplative power of hundreds of people in silent meditation; the way I had learned to trust my feelings rather than find them disturbing impediments to logic; the potential for extraordinary achievements by groups of everyday people who poured their hearts into noble initiatives; countless moments of delight amidst the constantly changing beauty of northern Scotland; and, of course, the tenderness of friends and lovers. Carol, my poetic, Aikido black-belt girlfriend, was a very gifted intuitive who before coming to Scotland made an unorthodox living as a tealeaf reader in the teashops of Boston. She, the whole Findhorn community, and I shared a commitment to creating a better world and doing what we could to create a model for the future.

As I stood on the station platform at Forres waiting for my train to London, three-and-a-half years after my first arrival, a total of 100 pounds and a one-way ticket to America in my pocket, I had few regrets. Findhorn was far from perfect — egos and political games were just as present as anywhere else — but I had seen that it was possible to build something fresh and ideal-istic that spoke to the yearnings in human hearts for community, love, and meaning. I had formed a group of friends that I knew would last a lifetime. I had glimpsed a sustainable technological future of solar energy, living machines, organic gardens, and coop-eration with nature. I had learned to love the fine, Zen-like quality of attention required by carpentry. I had cultivated deep peace in the sanctuaries meditating upon the patter of rain, the glints of sunlight, the scents of flowers and shrubs. And I deepened my love of nature in all its forms by coming to see the beauty in a sight as common as dew-covered purple cabbages radiant in the early-morning sun.

Destiny led me to a harder road than the warmth of commu-nity and the calm that comes from living close to nature. I was drawn back to the scope, size, and energy of America. It was there that my spiritual awakening had occurred, and it was there that the movement to awaken consciousness was most fully developed. I wanted to contribute to this, to pour my creativity, energy, and vision — now strengthened by my Findhorn experience — into this vast chalice. Ultimately, I felt America was at the heart of the struggle for the soul of humanity.

Through contacts made at Findhorn, I received an invitation to speak at a conference with the Onondaga leader Oren Lyons at the University of Wisconsin in Milwaukee in the fall of 1979. It came with a transatlantic ticket, and I knew this was my opportunity to begin the next phase of my life. But I was returning to a country where progress was less than certain. It was about to change presidents dramatically and begin a sustained engagement with turbo capitalism and the seductions of greed.

As the train pulled up at Forres Station and I stepped aboard, I felt the usual mix of anxiety and excitement that accompanies a new adventure. I was ready for more edge and societal engagement in my life, but Findhorn had deeply validated my vision of what was possible, and I reentered the world a little wiser and stronger and readier to do my bit in the great work of raising consciousness.

How the rest of my life would unfold was a complete mystery to me. I just knew that I had the desire to serve humanity. I didn't know how and I didn't know where, but I felt that America had the greatest concentration of people walking the path of alternative spirituality. My time in California still glowed in my memory, and Britain felt a bit too small, even though I deeply loved the Celtic fringe as a soul home closer to me by birth than any other part of the planet. I would miss the Scottish Highlands and Islands: their epic grandeur, their brooding history, their long summer days, and their ancient sense of soul. But my heart was drawn to the openness of America and its sense of spiritual dynamism. It was truly the "cradle of the best and the worst," in the words of Leonard Cohen. Some invisible thread drew me westward, and with an anxious feeling in the pit of my stomach and a grain of hope that new doors would open across the Atlantic, I boarded that train and watched the forests and fields beside the Moray Firth slip slowly behind me into the past.

CHAPTER SEVEN

∞

OMEGA INSTITUTE

HOLISTIC LEARNING'S EARLY YEARS

A fter Findhorn, I spent a long and difficult year and a half in California, mostly in Berkeley, trying to make money cleaning houses and weeding gardens. It was a rough transition. I had gone from serious contributor to planetary awakening to menial worker, sleeping on my friends' floor while I tried to figure out the next stage of my life. I did manage to make a bit of money picking pears and apples with mostly Mexican migrant workers in the Hood River Valley of Oregon, but it was exhausting work and extremely poorly paid. We had to fill a bin with 2,000 pears to make nine dollars while carrying a heavy sack around our necks, moving the ladder from tree to tree, and frequently balancing on one leg and stretching precariously to pick that final pear. It certainly changed my view of fruit the next time I saw it in a supermarket.

I spent the fall and winter of 1980–1981 commuting between Berkeley and the Hollywood Hills in Los Angeles, where I had found a new romance. Without a car, it was almost impossible to find work in L.A., so I gardened and cleaned in Northern California until I had enough money to live for three weeks or a month. Then I would catch a ride down through the flat, dry Central Valley to Hollywood and be with my lover Sharon until the money ran out and I had to return to my modest existence in the north.

It was a dreary and unfulfilling existence apart from the love dimension, which was full and deep. I was thirty years old, filled with vitality, and longing to be useful to the world at large. I had good and loyal friends in Berkeley, but this was no way to spend an incarnation. Life was not unfolding with the delicious synchronicity I had heard Peter Caddy describe so often. A number of times I was on the verge of leaving the States and returning to Europe or Canada, where things had to be better than the drudgery I was experiencing. In December 1980, I sent out cards to about twenty friends around the world, and it was this simple gesture that led to the next creative phase of my life. A few months later I received a call from Lucius, a Sufi friend living in upstate New York who had received one of my cards. He had become assistant program director of something called the Omega Institute for Holistic Studies, which presented workshops and short courses during the summer months in the Berkshire Mountains near the border of Massachusetts and New York. He told me that there were only two people in the programming department, they had both exhausted themselves the previous summer working nineteen-hour days for weeks on end, and he knew I had some experience at Findhorn overseeing educational programs. Would I be willing to come East for a summer and lend them a hand?

I rapidly agreed as I was in serious need of a new challenge and a more meaningful existence. In May I set out to drive across the country with my heart-centered girlfriend from the Hollywood Hills, expecting little more than an interesting summer. For the fourth summer in its modest existence, Omega had rented Bennington College in Vermont for its program and, while there were many excellent events, the distance from both New York and Boston was too great and there was a dramatic and potentially disastrous fall in registration numbers. It didn't help that the college food was appalling to participants who came expecting natural and organic vegetarian meals.

We had to share the campus with numerous other groups, including a group of writers who looked down their noses at us poor, deluded spiritual oafs lacking their acumen and intellectual rigor. In 1981, this group of "sophisticated" auteurs of literary America seemed to feel at best an amused tolerance and at worst a downright contempt for those of us embracing a holistic, spiritual worldview. It seemed to be the same old story of pitying those thought to be without the psychological strength to face up to their view of the inherent meaninglessness of the human condition.

I enjoyed being back in the fray again, but as summer drew to a close I needed to ponder my next step, which looked increasingly like a return to Europe. One afternoon I sat meditating on my future in the small house in a Vermont village that we had rented for the summer. As I went deeper into the silence, I suddenly experienced a remarkable clarity, an inner voice that was clear, strong, and compelling: "Relax, stay put; things will work out." I have rarely had such experiences in my life — but this was one of them, and I decided to pay attention. When I emerged from the silence, I was left with a powerful intuitive sense that the future would unfold in good time.

I told friends about my experience, and it became a source of some gentle amusement. As the final days of the summer program drew closer, people would ask me if I had made the big connection yet. Would it come with the next group of participants or the next set of teachers to arrive at Omega? But, sadly, the whole Institute wound up for the summer, no new avenues appeared magically, and I found myself packing my bags and wondering what would come next.

Then, a major disagreement exploded between the program and executive directors, and the former made an immediate decision to leave Omega and head for California. It had been a poor summer financially, and Omega was left with just enough money for one more roll of the dice, one more summer program that would have to be an outstanding success or the whole thing would be over. To my utter surprise, I wound up becoming the new program director, and suddenly the creative content of this valuable and potentially important place was largely in my hands and those of my colleague Ursula.

Omega has since become widely known in the eastern United States, but there was nothing glamorous about the job of program director when I took it in 1981. As Omega was originally an offshoot of the Abode of the Message Sufi community founded by Pir Vilayat Khan that was housed in a former Shaker village, its winter offices were located in the small town of Lebanon Springs nearby. Never in my life, not even in Huddersfield, have I been so bored. During that relentless, freezing winter of 1981, every evening after work I trudged in deep snow from our small office next to the post office to my cold and drafty apartment, which I shared with a young single mother and her frequently crying baby. We were all working for a pittance, and my girlfriend had returned to Los Angeles. I could only afford one long-distance call to her of an hour each week.

Hemmed in by the snow-covered hills with nothing but a grocery store and a dull bar for entertainment, there was nothing to do but watch television or read. Our tiny black-and-white set could only pick up one channel, so after the evening news, we were doomed to yet another showing of *Family Feud*. I knew this existence was starting to take its toll when Richard Dawson, the show's host, began to appear to me as a kind of Zen master. The nearest town was the very aptly named Pittsfield; when the weekly trip to its supermarket became the highpoint of my existence, the going had indeed become rough.

There were, however, compensations. My colleagues and I had a whole summer to fill with innovative programs, and America was bursting with new spiritual teachers, fresh psychological techniques, innovative approaches to bodywork, and a growing awareness of the value of alternative medicine. Shamans were emerging from the jungles of the Amazon; lamas appeared from remote monasteries in the Himalayas. Therapists were exploring the transpersonal dimensions of the psyche; African and Indian ritual dancers were starting to share their art forms.

Major honoraria were almost unknown in those days, so many teachers worked virtually for free. I could see from previous correspondence that my Sufi predecessors had addressed faculty as "Beloved Ones of God" and signed their letters "In the Light of the One." The noble idealism of the '70s was still in the air, and teaching on holistic topics had not yet become a growth industry. The lure of big money that poisoned the '80s, and changed the way holistic centers operated, was still to make an impact. The first yuppies had just been sighted, and few people imagined their values would become a prolonged fixture of the American scene.

As the scheduling boards filled up, a new problem asserted itself. Suddenly, we were without a home. As the printing deadline approached for the summer catalogue this was becoming serious. And then we discovered Camp Boiberik, a formerly Yiddish-speaking family camp near Rhinebeck, an hour and a half north of New York City.

I saw it first one snow-covered day with leaden skies. Eighty-six buildings on a hundred and eight acres, almost all of them neglected, many with collapsed and leaking roofs. A stench emanated from the kitchen where the previous owners had abandoned many cans of food that had exploded in the summer heat. I yanked open the half-rusted door of the pantry and found myself staring at a large rat, up on its hind legs, its yellow teeth exposed. I slammed the door fast and sighed. Would it be possible for a single decent meal ever to emerge from a place like this, let alone to run a program serving thousands of people? Upon further investigation, we discovered that it took roughly half an hour for hot water to make its way from the aged boiler to the farthest cabins. How would that go down with demanding New Yorkers? At least at Cluny Hill there was a community of hundreds to assist in the cleanup and renovation. Here we had a year-round staff of seven or eight, and the task was equally (if not more) formidable.

I began to have fantasies of participants en masse demanding their money back and the whole summer becoming a total fiasco with me as the front man. Just my luck to become program director in the midst of a crisis. On top of this, I didn't really know what a summer camp was, having grown up in Europe. An old comical hit record I knew from the early '60s — "Hello muddah, hello fadduh / Here I am at Camp Granada," began to play in my head with all its evocation of adolescent horror. This was looking decidedly grim.

But the alternatives were few and equally risky. The catalogue deadline was almost upon us, Darrow School was adamant about refusing to take us back, and those who knew what a camp looked like in the summer thought we were in with a fighting chance. Lease for the summer with an option to buy, if we survived! At least the place was dirt cheap. Like Cluny Hill, it was another white elephant in the eyes of the conventional real-estate market. I learned later that Camp Boiberik had a distinguished history earlier in the century as a center of Yiddish culture, but little of that was evident in the space we took over in 1981.

As Memorial Day approached, the work became increasingly frantic. There was only time to paint the front of selected buildings, rebuild broken roofs and porches, carpet the meeting-room floors, rename the buildings in the holistic spirit (usually after trees), and keep our fingers crossed. The brochure, in a careful display of understatement, had described the facility as "rustic," and we could only hope that participants would not be demanding refunds and hurling tomatoes at the hapless organizers, some of whom retained half-serious contingency plans to disappear out the back door and hit the road in a cloud of dust before the yelling mobs wreaked havoc. The day before the summer opened, I stood on top of a ladder putting the last touches on the painting of the Main Hall, and on the transition from Camp Boiberik to Omega Institute for Holistic Studies.

At that point, there were few advocating for new centers from which cultural renewal could emanate. Could there really be a serious interest in places like that? The people who arrived the next day seemed to think so. They wanted the freedom to discover a spirituality that was alive, fresh, relevant, deep, and inclusive, and the chance to experience, at least for five days or a long weekend, a warm sense of community with others who shared their holistic values. And that's exactly what they got. To my immense relief, people loved the place despite its semi-ramshackle dimension and infrequent hot-water supply. The chance to create our own space from scratch more than made up for the physical limitations. The rotten old deck was hauled out of the lake; the kitchen started knocking out decent vegetarian food; the crowds extended great understanding for our predicament; and registration soared. As for me, I started running in May, and didn't stop until September. We had just enough chairs for each new round of guests; at every program turnover, each Friday and Sunday, my colleague Steven and I had to pick them all up, stash them in his van, and redistribute them all over campus. The logistics were a nightmare, but before long we began to believe that this thing was actually working.

It was not an intentional community like Findhorn. Instead, it was an institute for holistic learning teaching the methods, practices, and philosophies of an emerging worldview filled with life and vitality. My memories are filled with images of attractive young people, scantily clad in their summer shorts and tank tops, listening with total attention to elderly Chinese tai chi teachers, professors of nutrition, masters of iridology, and Tibetan doctors. Or bodies shaking to the rhythms of Indian temple dance and African movement, and sitting quietly in the lotus position as Native American chiefs, elders, and pipe carriers described their ancient traditions and their value today. It gave me immense pleasure to provide a forum for the native peoples — the Sacred Circle, as we called it — whose profound attunement to the wisdom of the earth had been devastated so painfully by European greed. The whole summer passed by in a riot of appreciative people, eccentric teachers, opening hearts, overwhelming good humor, and the occasional inadvertent comedy when a self-important guru would reveal his inflated ego while lecturing on the transcendence of self.

I recall one Korean Zen master and his shaven-headed acolytes making their first visit to Omega. During a panel on the world's mystical traditions that I was moderating, he rambled endlessly in English that was disturbingly indecipherable, taking inordinate time from the other speakers from the Christian, Hindu, Sufi, and Jewish traditions. In those days, if someone was designated a Zen master or Tibetan lama, I had such profound respect for them that I censored my own instincts when it came to appropriate behavior. I thought that they probably knew something I didn't, and cut them a lot of slack. But in this instance, the outsize ego was unmistakable. Eventually, I just waited for him to run out of breath, and jumped in while he was inhaling. Fortunately, there were not too many of these experiences. My training at Findhorn had given me a fine eye for spiritual baloney, and our effort was always to keep the programs authentic, unpretentious, and grounded.

Omega's approach allowed participants to focus on their primary interest in the morning, and then taste some of the other course offerings in the afternoon. This enabled many people to discover entirely fresh disciplines and holistic techniques. But something else occurred in the dining room or the café, on walks through the campus between sessions, or while lounging at the lake. It was the chance to connect deeply with people of like mind. So many unconventionally spiritual people rarely had the chance to meet others. They were perhaps the only person in their families with this disposition, or maybe there was no one else at work with whom they could share their perspective. So the social dimension of a holistic center is vital to its work. On countless occasions, strangers meeting for the first time across a lunch table found a strong sense of resonance with each other. People from the same profession discovered others with the same instinct for new directions in the field. And, of course, love also bloomed. The romantic dimension to a center's work can never be forgotten if we adopt a truly holistic understanding of what is required to address the whole person.

Lives were changed, partnerships formed, inspirations encouraged, and new professional groupings seeded. And this is true of all holistic centers that work effectively. We need venues in which people with the vision and desire to transform society meet each other and recognize potential colleagues in the work. In this way, regenerative impulses in fields like business, law, medicine, nursing, psychotherapy, and education can find their way forward. For the organizers of a center, it is immensely satisfying to see this process at work in the hum of the dining room or the absorbing conversation after a workshop.

Holistic learning centers are generators of a new conscious-ness. In the early '80s, it was time to create coherent alternatives that would gradually penetrate mainstream culture over the coming decades. Omega had emerged from the Sufi tradition, but it was philosophically eclectic. We aimed to show the mystical unity at the heart of world religions, and that good health came from the harmony of body, mind, and spirit, not just innovations in medical technology. We held out to our participants the oppor-tunity to delight in the endlessly creative rhythms of world music, dance, and drumming that we embraced on equal par with the culture of Europe, and to heal the psychological wounds between mothers and daughters, fathers and sons. We wanted to delve into states of consciousness beyond the normal and find the wisdom in mythologies and shamanic journeys that had long been cast aside as primitive superstition by a West convinced of its intellectual superiority, but unconscious of the cultural desert forming in its midst that was parching the souls of its citizens.

These were the early days of Jon Kabat-Zinn and his pioneering approach to mindfulness meditation and health; of dancers bringing their hypnotic steps and rhythms to a youthful audience eager for new moves; of psycho-synthesis and its concept of sub-personalities and the higher self.

For me, the highlight of the first summer in Rhinebeck was the Way of Social Action, a week I organized with Ram Dass and the leaders of Greenpeace, Amnesty International, and Oxfam. For years I had seen the need to bring together the mystical and spiritual dimensions of the world with the socially, politically, and environmentally engaged. Too often, it seemed to me, those on the spiritual path immersed themselves in practices and meditations that left them oblivious to the injustices of the world. This week, however, blew away any traces of New Age narcissism and firmly grounded post-psychedelic spirituality in the issues and suffering of humanity and the earth. Now *that* was true holistic thinking!

If the exploration of the further reaches of the inner world could lead us ultimately to deeper engagement with the needs of the outer world, the circle of wholeness would be complete, and we could feel that we were generating a worldview that was genuinely life sustaining. The Way of Social Action fulfilled that mission for the hundred or so participants, and left me with a profound sense of satisfaction. I was doing the work I was meant to do on this earth, and bit by bit, the awakening of consciousness was taking place.

Omega had somehow become an oasis offering the waters of life, of meaning, of deeper truth in a society increasingly caught in an excess of work, stress, and a glut of shallow stimulation. It wasn't the established institutions that offered renewal at such a moment. What was needed was something unhampered by the overspecialization of academia or the perceived conventionality of church and synagogue. Somehow it fell to a rather ragged group of idealistic characters making it all up as they went along — but young, energetic, and hopeful. There were many stumbles and painful moments as egos clashed and power trips loomed. But people needed holistic centers, a new spirit was abroad in the land, and a collection of spiritual misfits once more turned a crumbling relic into a place of inspiration.

When the time came for me to leave Omega after two-and-a-half years, I could look back on a pivotal era that had begun to establish the Institute on a path of sustainability. There were many more rivers to cross, but I had a thousand memories of seeing an old ramshackle camp come alive with new vitality and of witnessing thousands of people enter with delight into new fields of knowledge in health, psychology, spirituality, ecology, and the arts. Many would go on to open clinics or develop therapy practices that served their communities. Others simply found ways to cultivate inner peace or discovered spiritual answers to nagging questions and doubts. Still more found a nourishing set of values and a community that expressed them.

As for me, I had found work that brought me personal satisfaction. I could serve humanity while staying true to my inner vision, and I could play a valuable role in the renewal and regeneration of our moribund culture. It had been a long way from the mountaintops of the Andes to the Hudson River Valley, from cosmic vision to grounded practice, from mystical experience of the One to intense engagement in the multiple details of running the programs of a vital and successful center. But the consistent theme for my own life was clear and enduring.

There was a vast but subtle awakening happening even if it was imperceptible to many. The yearning in the human heart for greater meaning, for community, for attunement to the earth, and for the embrace of all peoples was beginning to happen. Centers of consciousness like Omega and Findhorn, scattered and few though they were, served as beacons drawing those who longed for paths of wisdom and new ways to serve the world. Thousands came and were refreshed and inspired.

But for many, the dreaded journey back to the "real world" always loomed — back to the big cities, the rush and stress, the anxiety and competition, the poverty and violence. Was it possible to bring this holistic approach to learning and growth into the dense urban morass of contemporary America? Could a city as formidable as New York ever provide fertile ground for these tender new shoots of awareness? As the last week of the Omega summer came to an end, I had no idea that Manhattan was about to take a firm grip on my life, and that my next step would be no less than full-scale immersion in the intense spiritual struggles of the most demanding and influential city of them all.

∞

CHAPTER EIGHT

SPIRIT IN THE CITY

NEW YORK AND ITS
OPEN CENTER

As the train from Rhinebeck made its way south down the tracks by the Hudson River, I began to make out the city skyline of New York. First it was the Bronx, with its rundown buildings and desperate feeling; then, away in the distance, I saw the towers, pinnacles, and spires of Manhattan. A sense of the weight of the challenge began to oppress me. Here I was, taking on the formidable task of creating a center for new spirituality and culture in the midst of one of the most powerful vortices of influence and energy on earth.

You must be joking! I thought when I pondered that I was a mere thirty-two and was not even an American, let alone a New Yorker. The conventional wisdom in 1983 was that a holistic center would never work in New York. "Come on! This is the *real* world. Maybe in California or Hawaii, but not here. Besides, if New York needed one, it'd already have one." I heard these sentiments many times in the early months, but we pressed on, undeterred.

On Christmas Day the previous year I had met with Walter Beebe, a partner in a Wall Street law firm and a man who made a decision in midlife to make a new kind of contribution to society. He was a member of a group that had emerged with the intention of creating a holistic center in the city. Initially, the thought had been that it would provide office space for many smaller spiritual and holistic initiatives, but it soon became clear to me that something more was needed: a focal point for the new awareness, an oasis, a haven, a place that would say very clearly that New York, the biggest, baddest city in America, was filled with people who yearned for an alternative spirituality and something deeper than the secular materialism of the mainstream intellectual establishment.

Over the years of searching, through the countless experiences of seeing groups of strangers transformed into loving, caring units bursting with warmth for each other, I had gained the conviction that centers of new consciousness were needed all over the world. Something in my own destiny drew me to the darker corners of the human experience, like the urban grimness of Chicago, Bogotá, and New York. I also loved life among the flowers and vegetables of Findhorn or the peace and beauty of British Columbia. Always in me there has been a war between the desire for life in the slow lane and life in the fast lane. I wanted serenity and transcendence, but I also wanted edge, pace, excitement, stimulation, and the feeling of being at the center of things.

Too often at Findhorn, I had been disturbed by the naïveté of members about the world at large. In order for this holistic spirituality to be taken seriously, I knew it had to penetrate into the belly of the material world, into the buzz, the speed, and the stress at the center of modern life. So often I had heard about new heart, new energy, and new vision awakened in rural centers and retreats in places of beauty. But then came the dreaded return to the place of work and the soul-deadening ambience of consumer capitalism — the notorious "real world," where fragile new hopes and dreams could be crushed so quickly and easily. Then the beautiful vision began to seem like a hopeless quest, and the aspiring soul was sucked back into the dreary banality of the everyday struggle for money and survival.

The Open Center, however, had the potential to be something different. There would be no "real world" to dread. Participants would already be there. There was just one catch: We actually had to do the long, hard work of creating a center of holistic learning right in the middle of New York's mean streets. And back in 1983, they were really mean.

For me, personally, moving to New York was not the fulfill-ment of a lifelong dream. My first glimpse of the city had been a horribly hot and muggy September day back in 1970 when the humid air was thick and unbreathable; curious and unap-pealing smells pervaded many street corners; and harried, anxious, and sweaty people poured from countless doorways. Why on earth would anyone choose to live in a place so obvi-ously difficult and uncomfortable? When I had passed through the city in years past, it was at the nadir of its financial woes. The violence was rising; the subways were graffiti-covered, ugly, and dangerous; and punks were gathering in the East Village to view with relish the cult classic *Escape from New York* in which Manhattan had become a giant prison camp. Reality didn't seem all that different.

Take me to the cool and mystical Celtic climes, or to sunny, enlightened California. Take me anywhere, in fact, other than this overcrowded, angry, rude, and chaotic place that millions of poor benighted souls had somehow convinced themselves was the center of the universe.

Thus, starting the Open Center was hardly my dream job. On the other hand, I have always been drawn to things out on the edge of the possible. "Beaten paths are for beaten men" were the words of Dane Rudhyar that had long resonated with me. To start the Open Center was to engage in a kind of spiritual "mission impossible." On the other hand, if it were true for Frank Sinatra when he sang, "If I can make it there, I'll make it anywhere," then surely it would be true for the creation of a viable and enduring holistic center. Perhaps in creating the Open Center we would be doing something not just for New York, but for the whole world too. If a center could work there, then why not also in Siberia or Rio or Sydney?

What were these centers at the deepest level? Places where people's lives were changed. Everything had to begin with the individual. In the deepest recesses of his or her heart, in the most private place of the psyche, a new sense of the possible could come into being. Yes, books could and did change many individuals, but a center in which the finest authors and teachers of the holistic worldview could speak to receptive audiences would complement the power of the book.

This was the dream, but we had a long way to go to get there. I barely knew a soul in New York. A few contacts from Findhorn and some acquaintances from Omega were my only points of reference. For my first few months in the city, an acquaintance offered me a small apartment on Bleecker Street in Greenwich Village. After the dreary tedium of winter life in Lebanon Springs in upstate New York, I wanted somewhere fun and active. But I wasn't sure I wanted the loud nightclubs till four in the morning, the relentless street traffic, and the peculiar fatigue that the city induced in those used to personal replenishment from fresh air, forests, and open skies. After years in the country I found the city draining and without places of sanctuary. Yet I loved the multiethnicity and the babble of languages, the throb and hum of raw urban life, the sense that every experience conceived by the human mind was available twenty-four hours a day for anyone with the time, energy, money, and madness to pursue it. It was a long way from the narrow world of Huddersfield where so often as a teenager I had imagined escaping to a fuller, more adventurous life. But it felt formidable and exhausting as I pondered how to begin.

Could we really help to bring the love, the wisdom, the energy, and the beauty of far northern Scotland, of hidden recesses in the Hudson River Valley, into this harsh and demanding place? Would this work, or was it just a quixotic gesture soon to be overwhelmed by the fierce realities of this legendarily tough and hard-edged city? Certainly, it would work only if the universe saw fit to conspire in our favor and the people and resources came together to make the dream possible.

Walter was an interesting and unique person. Son of the former president of the Washington Post Company, educated at Harvard and Stanford Law School, well versed in the rigors of corporate law — what on earth was he doing trying to start a center with such impossible aspirations?

When Walter first invited me to the Stock Exchange for breakfast, the maître d' had to loan me a yellow, polka-dot tie so that I could be served. Talk about a fish out of water! I felt that I had entered the lair of the enemy as I sat in my borrowed jacket and hiking boots surveying the assembled brokers and executives. Back then people with my political bent found the whole world of Wall Street impossibly distant and strange. No one imagined that the computerized trading of stocks would soon become an activity for everyman; then, the denizens of this rarified world looked only a tad different from the top-hatted capitalists of caricature to my wide eyes.

Yet this was the world from which Walter had emerged with a desire to support the new spirituality. His first wife had introduced him to the inner journey, and Jean Houston had served as an intellectual guide and inspiration as he faced the questions of midlife. Walter's commitment was genuine, and I learned the valuable lesson that noble intentions could emerge even from the most unlikely centers of financial and corporate power. My life over the previous dozen years had left me distant from the world of big money and deeply skeptical of its intentions.

Many centers in the '70s had started on a shoestring, but this would never work in New York City. Walter's resources, aided by a stroke of good luck on the market, made the acquisition of a building in a neglected corner of the city possible. He and I looked at many sites, but when we found a modern architect's office on an obscure block of Spring Street in SoHo, I knew we had stumbled on something special. Linda, my girlfriend at that time and an early supporter of the idea of the Open Center, was a real-estate broker. After a long and dedicated search, she finally found a building with real potential. Her creativity, insight, and artistic eye were invaluable in the Open Center finding its home. On the ground floor was the design room, on the second the exhibition of architectural models, on the third an unrelated toy factory. It was hardly the obvious choice for a holistic center, but by the time we emerged onto the roof, my mind was awhirl, spinning with images, ablaze with feelings of potential.

It had a feeling of lightness and openness, despite the narrow width of the building. The whole look was modern, bright, and creative, and had been designed by the well-known architect, James Wines, as the home of his company, Sculpture in the Environment. Walter and I could easily imagine lectures and concerts on the ground floor, and there was even a little nook that would work perfectly for a meditation room. I felt we needed a place devoted exclusively to silence somewhere in the building for the sake of our own sanity and inner connection. And it was close to a lot of subway stops for easy access. The whole atmosphere felt exactly right. This surely was the space we needed.

In the meantime, we had to construct a program. Returning in March 1983 from a winter break with friends in Key West, I calculated that we could, if all things went well, open our doors in nine months. Over the winter, I had worked on creating the summer programs for Omega; I would have to return to Rhinebeck to run them in June. But now I had three months in the city to invent the contents of the very first Open Center catalogue. Who should I contact first? Sitting in Walter's home on Twelfth Street that had become our temporary office, my thoughts drifted naturally to David Spangler. From my time at Findhorn, I knew him to be a person of integrity and genuine spiritual vision. I wanted both those qualities to imbue our fledgling center. I also wanted to avoid the New Age flakiness that was the curse of independent spirituality. We didn't need channelers, crystal healers, and self-proclaimed emissaries of the hierarchy of masters. We needed authentic spiritual substance, attuned to higher worlds, but in a manner that was grounded and astute. We needed a view of the human psyche that acknowledged its darker shadow dimensions as befit the suffering and pain that surrounded us in the city. Jung's understanding of the shadow was never far from my mind in those early months.

We also needed a program that honored the Western spiritual paths as well as the Eastern. So many alternative centers focused primarily on Buddhism, yoga, shiatsu, and other Asian approaches to contemplation and wellness. While I had immense respect for these traditions, I felt the Open Center should also aim to bring mystical Christian, Judaic, hermetic, and alchemic insights into a more prominent place in the panoply of holistic spirituality. We should honor and enjoy the cultural diversity of New York, the full spectrum of its multicultural wealth, with the music, art, and spirituality of the African and Latino populations. And we needed to engage with the outer world as well as the inner. As far as I was concerned, the holistic impulse was as much about changing the environment, the economy, and society as it was about changing ourselves. Yes, transformation began in the inner self and often led to a long inner journey that could take years or decades and was never fully complete. But what was the point of this awakening of consciousness if its fruits were never returned to the world? An exclusive concentration on the inner life might be appropriate for rural retreat centers focused on personal renewal, but for an inner-city center that aimed to be relevant, contemporary, and innovative, there was an imperative to deal directly with the world. How could the non-materialistic values, the love of nature, the lessons of ecology, the respect for all beings, and the honoring of the divinity at the heart of all people play out in relation to economics, the media, even political life? These were the questions, it seemed to me, with which a New York Open Center had to engage.

But first we had to assemble a team willing to take on this madcap task. The first colleague for Walter and me was the irrepressible Sandy. Blond, upbeat, ever optimistic, and possessed of a truly golden heart, she had emerged from a career in magazines to find herself unexpectedly available for our venture. With Walter's knowledge of real estate, law, and business, and my grasp of the subjects, teachers, and themes of the holistic world, we needed a balancing female element whose constant emphasis on the heart and human relationships never wavered.

Initially, we didn't even have a typewriter, let alone a computer. I had to shout down the stairs to Cathy, Walter's teenage daughter, to see if I could borrow the small, plastic machine she was using to learn to type before I could send an invitation letter to any presenter. At the end of his workday, Walter would return from his law firm and join Sandy and me in his front room to ponder the day's progress. Sometimes the task seemed overwhelming and impossible; other times it seemed filled with hope and potential. I had already poured so much of my creative energy into the Omega summer programs looming in the distance. Now I had to find the resources and depth of inspiration to create a program that would launch us with a splash and show our audience that we were serious and here to stay.

Serendipity played a big role in all of this. One time, when visiting Kanya KeKhumba of UCLA (the University at the Corner of Lennox Avenue), our primary contact in Harlem, I met a young tai chi practitioner named Yosef. He became the center's teacher in this field. Mostly I invited speakers from far afield for the weekend programs who had impressed me with their teaching or writing. But the local teachers who would offer the ongoing evening programs were usually just folks I had met around town as I explored this vast urban world. Gradually, the creative content of the Open Center began to take shape, and the time approached when I needed to return to Omega to run the summer programs. As usual with Omega's tiny programming team, we started running in June and didn't stop until September. It was an exhilarating and highly successful summer of nonstop activity, improvisation, and focus. At the end, I knew that the move to the former Camp Boiberik with all its risks had proven a success, and that Omega was well launched in its new home. As Labor Day rolled around, I could feel the ending of an era in my life. Goodbye to the hectic summers and cold, snowy, endless upstate winters. Farewell to the Sufi and the strange, semi-desolate world of Lebanon Springs. I was thirty-four years old, a new phase of my life was beginning, and all my youthful powers were needed as I headed to the big city to pull the new center together in time for the New Year.

1984 was coming up fast, and the Orwellian overtones loomed large. It was formidable enough to take on New York at any time, but this particular year seemed especially foreboding. Was it all just a misplaced fantasy, or could this Open Center really make a difference? The densest spots could hardly be immune. Ultimately, they were the places that needed it most, but there were not many blueprints how to do it. The Cambridge / Boston area had an admirable facility, Project Interface, and the '60s had seen the appearance of an earlier, more stoned version of a center in Amsterdam's Der Kosmos. But Cambridge was the academic capital of America and was filled with intelligent, aware people. *New Age Journal* was there to support and inspire Project Interface, with its contacts and mailing lists. Amsterdam was, well, Amsterdam, and the most open-minded city in Europe with a unique level of relaxation and support for alternative culture.

New York at that time had upward-spiraling crime statistics, a tense racial situation, and major areas that no sane white person would visit alone after dusk. It seemed to be descending further into chaos on the street. Fear and danger were certainly in the air.

As I sat in Greenwich Village pondering this, I was grateful to Michael Murphy and Dick Price for having founded Esalen in the gorgeous Pacific world of Big Sur, and thankful to Peter and Eileen Caddy and Dorothy Maclean for having established Findhorn in a corner of northern Scotland filled with serenity and beauty. I was really glad that Pir Vilayat Inayat Khan and Stefan and Elizabeth Rechtschaffen had enabled Omega to take its first steps into incarnation in upstate New York. Now it somehow fell to me and my small group of colleagues to bring a coherent vision of a new way of being to the archetypal big city of the modern world.

I felt up for the challenge, ready to go for it, glad that destiny had brought me to this moment, amazed at the task before us, and stunned by the mysterious working of karma that brought a lad from Wales and Huddersfield to this hugely creative point. But I couldn't escape a hint of trepidation, a little tightening of the solar plexus, a few moments of doubt about the dream of global awakening, and a sense that this was about to be one of the most challenging and stretching experiences of my whole life.

When I returned to New York in September, we worked in earnest on creating the team to run the center. Our first piece of good luck was the appearance of Sam, our program coordinator, who had come East after twelve years work in the Grand Canyon as a river-raft guide and ranger. Unflappable, resourceful, and a practicing Tibetan Buddhist, Sam was used to handling times of great stress like roaring whitewater rapids and people falling out of rafts in churning currents. He was just the man to oversee the execution of events.

Clare, my new love partner, was a very quick, smart, on-top-of-it administrator who had just completed a master's degree in holistic education. She was the kind of person who in her youth could party all night, stumble into a temp agency in the morning, ace all their tests for typing and office skills, and wind up being offered the most demanding jobs that others worked in vain to attain for months. She had a comfort level in dealing with the mainstream world that most of us lacked as a result of her free and varied lifestyle in which she had worked with the National Association of Trial Lawyers and other groups far from the alternative world. Although always, like me, a bohemian at heart, she had picked up an impressive range of skills and a level of professional competence that were perfect for us as our team of misfits began to jell into a coherent whole.

At last, the first catalogue neared completion. I sat alone in our second-floor office composing the first vision statement with which it would begin. Time now to convey the essence of our project to the masses of New Yorkers — time to show that we had sincerity and vision, and that those thousands of city dwellers who had pondered and practiced their holistic values alone for so long could now find a place of refuge devoted to the ideals they held close to their hearts.

The moment of truth was approaching. Would we fall flat on our faces and stand exposed as naïve dreamers, out of touch with the nature of the real world? Or would we generate a grateful response, a sigh of relief, a sense that New York now had its own center for this new consciousness that remained so invisible to the establishment media and academia?

The need for a spiritual revitalization of the culture was undeniable. But sustained renewal would not come from the established institutions. The universities and the mainstream media were too implicated in the old order. Our task was to construct and maintain nodes of cultural regeneration. Change would come, as it always had, from free individuals able to think outside conventional limits and willing to trust their hearts.

We now needed a registrar to take the first phone calls we hoped would come in abundance when the new catalogue landed in mailboxes. I turned to a reliable source — my old colleague, the shy and humble Charles from Findhorn. He was dutifully installed in his basement office on Spring Street with one phone line, no call-waiting, and a pad of paper to take names and addresses. Finally, as the prospect of actually opening our doors grew closer, we needed a receptionist; a young woman from Syracuse, Adele, whose smooth voice and manner on the phone had impressed me a few days earlier, joined us and became a central and valued member of our team. Not long after, Ron, a feisty and dedicated Vietnam vet, brought his considerable charm and gifts to our incipient efforts at outreach and public relations, and our original team was complete.

Now for the actual start. Our opening event was held on the bitter Friday night of January 13, 1984. Could dates and times have conspired to produce a moment more perfect for trepidation and anxiety? It was a concert by Paul Winter premiering his new album *Sun Singer* at Cooper Union, the historic auditorium where Abraham Lincoln had spoken. Would anybody show up? Would they take us for fools? To our delight, we sold the whole place out, there were huge cheers from the audience for our new project, and we launched with a spirit that was heartwarming and enormously validating.

Thank God, because in the long, frigid winter that followed, only one evening course reached double figures in the number of participants. Many icy evenings, I stood on the fire-escape stairs outside the third-floor classroom peering in vain into the darkness of SoHo, hoping that another attendee would come 'round the corner. At that time, all the buildings on the block were jet black with soot, the streetlights worked intermittently, what is now a leading natural-food restaurant was a methadone clinic for heroin addiction, and there were no stores or businesses on lower Broadway that were open in the evening to provide a sense of light and safety. What is today Balthazar's Restaurant was a small center of the leather industry run by Hasidic gentlemen very focused on their own world, and most people ambled by our block unconscious of anything interesting on it. We were easily overlooked, lost in a no-man's-land somewhere between Broadway and Little Italy.

Our one successful evening program was a series of lectures given by City University of New York philosophy professor Robert McDermott, later president of the California Institute of Integral Studies. He called it "Modern Masters," and it was perfect for our first lecture series. He covered Jung, Steiner, Aurobindo, Buber, and Gandhi; by its end, I could already feel a new canon, a new pantheon of intellectual and spiritual heroes, emerging to give substance to the Open Center. These were the kinds of writers and thinkers we embraced — each had profound insight into the deeper realities beneath the surface of life, and a concept of how we could move the world in directions more befitting human dignity and hope. This was a firm intellectual foundation upon which to build a life-enhancing culture. The Open Center would never be engaged exclusively with one path or one discipline. Instead, it would find the best and the deepest sources of renewal that the world could offer. From a modest, five-story building on Spring Street, influences radiated to whomever among the sixteen million people within a one-hour radius was open and willing to listen.

Some months later, I stood on Spring Street on a Friday night gazing in meditation at the Open Center. On the third floor, the psychologist Sam Keen was speaking on the shadow we were projecting onto the Soviet Union with all its attendant propaganda and distortion. In the teahouse on the ground floor, there was a jazz concert with Paul McCandless and his band on woodwind instruments, echo-chamber guitar, vibes, percussion, and keyboards. This is what I want, I thought; this is what the Open Center's here to offer: high-quality presentations of intellectual substance that address the intersection of soul and society, and superb artistic events that are hip, rhythmic, evocative, and transcendent. That night I knew that we were on track, and that the beautiful vision was inch by inch, step by step on its way to becoming reality.

The next four years were a time of exhilaration, exhaustion, warm comradeship, pushing myself to the limit, and a growing sense of achievement. Throughout those early years, the only way to find the peace and quiet to write the catalogues was to work at night, often with my old-soul friend Dennis, who was doubling as registrar. I had known Dennis since Findhorn, and our natural spiritual resonance and easy friendship were truly valuable. For every deadline until 1988, I would work all night at the deserted Open Center, editing course descriptions, describing programs, concocting social events, trying to put concepts into coherent and clear prose.

As dawn broke, I emerged blinking into the sun and made my way west on Spring Street to the apartment that I shared with Clare. Often I would pause at the corner of Spring and West

Broadway, where there was a perfect view of both the Empire State Building to the north and the World Trade Center towers to the South. In the dawn sunshine they looked beautiful, and I would pause in a moment of wonder and gratitude that I had been given the privilege to help create this center of consciousness and sacred wisdom at the pulsating heart of the modern world. Standing equidistant between the great towers, experiencing a semi-altered state of consciousness in my fatigue and sleeplessness after long hours of concentration, I felt a kind of karmic blessing that it had fallen to me to pour my very lifeblood, so much of my youthful vitality, into the noble dream of our Open Center, and that it appeared to be working. I was grateful to be fully engaged with something that corresponded to my ideals, amazed that we were doing this work slap bang in the middle of New York City. In that clear-eyed state that can follow extreme exhaustion after a week of working all night, I felt grateful for the gift of total creative freedom to shape the direction and content of the center's activities.

So many memories flood back from the early days of the Open Center. A source of special joy to me was when my parents came over to New York. It had been five or six years since I had last seen them, and now I could invite them into my life and its work. My father, in particular, had never had much time for any of this spiritual stuff, and there were few holistic traces in Huddersfield, but our first New Year's party was a moment of healing and grace for the family. It was the end of an arduous and highly successful year. It was time to celebrate with intense exhilaration, and I was delighted to invite my parents into my world. My father had suffered a very painful leg fracture some months earlier that had caused him real suffering and depression. At last, I felt that I could give him something at this boisterous, ecstatic conclusion to the year. And indeed, he found the perfect role serving champagne after midnight with his boyish smile. I began to feel for the first time that he might have some sympathy and understanding for the work to which I had devoted my life. That night was a healing from years of awkward and distant feeling. I felt recognized and acknowledged, and there was a renewed connection with my parents by the time they returned to England.

Something else caught my notice at the party. A group of eight single women had arrived with the large crowd early in the evening, and every single one of them had left with a date. From this I concluded that we had to be doing something right. Whenever eros visits an initiative unexpectedly, it is often a sign of blessing from life itself. A center is more than just a place where people acquire knowledge; it is also a focal point for love.

As for the team of dedicated colleagues who had come together to create the Open Center, we were moving steadily into a state of warm camaraderie. Of course there were tensions and disagreements, ego trips and accusations. But the overall tone was one of a special closeness that comes when we unite around a goal that speaks to our deepest aspirations and values. Many years later, when we met for a small reunion, there was that special joy that can sometimes come to those who have united their wills against the grain of conventional attitudes to create something society really needs.

The '80s at the Open Center were a joyful and fulfilling time for me. I worked insane hours, virtually lived at the place, did most of the programming, wrote most of the catalogues, did a lot of the management and administration, and introduced almost all of the speakers. But the feeling inside was one of satisfaction. Thousands of participants were coming, and attendance was growing steadily. Income was climbing in a steep curve that made the project seem increasingly viable. We organized the first New York conferences on socially responsible investing and the destruction of the rainforests. We created a program that was intellectually rigorous, socially engaged, and spiritually cosmopolitan, and before the decade was out we had established ourselves as a vital center with a growing reputation in North America and worldwide. A steady flow of visitors asked to meet with Walter and myself to ask how we had done it and how they might do something similar in cities all over the planet. As I had surmised, the sheer fact of our continuing existence in New York seemed to offer a note of hope and inspiration to many individuals who wanted to contribute to a change in consciousness. I was doing the work for which I had been born, and it was making a difference in a place that counted.

When the phone rang, I never knew who would be on the other end. Would it be a lama from Tibet, a shaman from the Amazon, the creator of a new bodywork method from California, an environmental activist, even a poet from the Celtic world? Or would it be some determined New York holistic hustler who wanted his course in our increasingly visible catalogue and wouldn't take no for an answer? I certainly had to exercise all the powers of discernment that years of exposure to spiritual teachers, psychologists, and healers of all stripes had given me. It was crucial to keep out the fluff, the New Age fantasists, those who, though well intentioned, only undermined the credibility so essential to the emerging holistic, ecological impulse. And it was hard to say no to so many goodhearted people.

Eventually, I began to feel that I had achieved what I came to New York for. The Center was on a roll, our reputation was high, enrollment was increasing, and we had a dedicated and heart-centered staff. But I was tired, fried, used up, and deeply in need of long strolls down deserted beaches and silent treks deep into remote mountains. After five years of nonstop work on the Open Center, and two and a half before that at Omega, I knew it was time for a rest. All my life I had carried the dream of traveling around the world, of seeing the traces of ancient Egypt, the mysteries of India, and the snowcaps of the Himalayas. I wanted to swim on the beaches of Bali, snorkel on the Great Barrier Reef of Australia. By early 1988, I knew it was time for a break.

As my feet stepped outside 83 Spring Street, I was filled with gratitude and a sense of mission achieved. Who knew what the future might hold for the Open Center, or for me? All I knew was that it was time to step away, replenish my reserves, and rekindle my inspiration. After years spent working in one building, I wanted to embrace the planet, set out with a sense of limitless possibility, and see what doors destiny might open.

CHAPTER NINE

∽

A REQUEST FROM THE ORACLE OF TIBET

In February 1989, during a trip 'round the world after the first five exhilarating but exhausting years of the Open Center, I found myself in Dharamsala, India, staying at the Tibetan Nechung Monastery, home of the only functioning political oracle in the world. At certain ceremonial moments after lengthy ritual preparations, the monk serving as the vehicle for the oracle would go into trance wearing a heavy headdress and elaborate costume. Then he would dance and speak to the Kashag — the Tibetan parliament — and to the Dalai Lama himself. His words would offer advice on pressing political matters. This was a monastery with very few Westerners, and I was fortunate to spend a month there thanks to a personal connection.

It was the Tibetan New Year and the monks began their lengthy ceremony to invoke Pehar Gyalpo, the Nechung Chogyam, fierce protector of both Tibet itself and the Dalai Lama. I would wake in my small cell in the early, gray hour of the morning and hear the monks' prolonged, deep-baritone "Oms" interspersed with clashing cymbals and long trumpet blasts. This was a five-day ritual; as time went on, the rhythm became increasingly shamanic. Moved by this disciplined practice, I asked the monks if I would be permitted to join them for three mornings. They graciously agreed, and I sat quietly in a corner meditating while the ceremony continued — the celebrants in their high yellow hats and maroon robes, their enormous twelve-foot trumpets ready for use.

At the conclusion of the ritual, I was sitting in my room when a monk friend appeared at the door asking if he could bring the head monk inside. I was honored, and welcomed him. He sat down on the small bed next to mine and told the tale of his flight from Tibet. When the political and military situation came to a head in 1959, and the Dalai Lama fled across the mountains to India, the Chinese Communists wanted to capture the leaders of the Nechung Oracle very badly due to their important role in Tibetan political culture. A price had been placed on the head of the monk serving as the oracle and on the head monk himself, and both had been burned in effigy. They had barely escaped alive. As he spoke, I could feel the passion and outrage still burning beneath the head monk's composed and dignified bearing. I felt in him all the justified sorrow and anger at the way Chinese Communists had trashed the Tibetans' beautiful and ancient culture.

He reached the conclusion of his narrative and looked at me intensely. They had been waiting, he told me, for the right person to accomplish something of significance for the monastery. It was important to take some material into Tibet (to a place that I will leave unnamed). They felt I was the right person to do this. He had heard that I was planning to fly to Lhasa on the first plane of the year from Kathmandu. It was impossible for any Tibetan to carry this material, as they would be searched too thoroughly. Therefore the only chance lay with a Westerner. Would I be willing to do it?

I knew as soon as he spoke that I would, so I agreed with only a little hesitation. I had been fascinated by Tibet since childhood and had read my sister's copy of *Seven Years in Tibet* as a teenager. It had been important to me that the Open Center pioneered many programs on Tibetan spirituality and culture at a time when few knew or cared about the painful Tibetan predicament. And I had been touched by the spirit of Tibet during those deep meditations with the Nechung monks.

On the day before my departure, after a month in the monastery, the head monk returned to my room and placed the white *khata* silk scarf around my neck as a blessing. He refused all payment for my stay, and told me that while I was engaged in this attempt they would put me under the protection of the Nechung Chogyam. March 1989 was the thirtieth anniversary of the uprising against the Chinese that had led to the flight of the Dalai Lama. Protests had begun to occur in Lhasa, and news was appearing that monks were being shot dead at point-blank range simply for holding up a piece of cardboard on which a crude Tibetan flag had been drawn. Too much information was appearing in the world media about this official policy of "merciless repression." The borders of Tibet were sealed and all foreigners ordered out of the country in forty-eight hours. All flights to Lhasa were canceled, and it looked impossible to do what I had promised.

Then, one day in Kathmandu, I learned of the story of Joseph Rock, an Austrian-American explorer in the early twentieth century who had taken an obscure route into eastern Tibet in 1925 and written an article about it in an issue of that year's *National Geographic* entitled "The Land of the Yellow Lama." As far as I knew no one had followed this route since; it would mean entering eastern Tibet, or Kham, home of the fierce Khampa warriors who had defended the border of Tibet for a thousand years. These fighters had formed the core of the resistance to Mao's army for many years, and they did not conform to the conventional peace-loving image of Tibetans. With their powerful build, long, red-tasseled hair, cowboy hats, and big earrings, they were considered some of the finest horsemen in

Asia. They carried swords of varying length and were often crack shots. They had fought the Chinese in the 1950s and '60s from their home in the Four Rivers, Six Ranges region of eastern Tibet and, at high altitudes, man to man, they were considered unconquerable. That's why the major monasteries in Kham had been bombed, and countless atrocities committed against the innocent monks.

It was also why their home region was forbidden territory. From a copy of the *National Geographic* article given to me by a friend, which I devoured with fascination, it appeared that Joseph Rock, accompanied by a six-man armed guard, had crossed this remote mountain region infested with bandits and entered the Lama Kingdom of Muli, then one of the "least-visited places on earth." Not much had changed since in that respect.

I decided to give it a try. I now had a back door into Tibet, and although I knew this journey would be dangerous and lonely, it promised an unforgettable experience in the service of a good cause. I bought a secondhand backpack, a small tent, and some dehydrated food at a trekking shop in Nepal, and planned my journey. This would mean going to Bangkok and then flying to Kunming, the capital of Yunnan province in southwest China. From there I would need to make my way overland via Dali to Lijiang at the foot of the Tibetan snow range. From that point, all travel would have to be done without the knowledge or approval of the Chinese authorities. It looked risky and exhausting but fascinating.

I left Nepal on the first available flight to Bangkok. I had a few days to wait in Thailand for the weekly flight to Kunming, and already I could feel the knot in my solar plexus as I contemplated the journey ahead. Would I even get past customs and immigration on my arrival at Kunming Airport? When eventually I left

Bangkok in the very early morning, the sky was a distant pale blue with strange, disconcerting cloud formations. I felt very alone.

After a month spent around the Tibetan community, it was hard not to perceive China as a state possessed by the ugliest possible impulses. It felt like entering Mordor as we descended though the clouds. There was some kind of nerve-wracking confusion at customs, and then suddenly I was through. From there I took a long bus ride to the town of Dali, where I began to become familiar with the drab, almost inhuman nature of Communist architecture. Even the guesthouse felt like a prison with its grimy, unadorned walls. After months in India and Nepal surrounded by colorful images of deities, beautiful clothing, and gracious art, this was unbelievably ugly. The ubiquitous blue jackets and trousers of the people were depressing.

And then it was on to Lijiang, at the foot of the Tibetan snow range. Here I would make my final preparations. But something unexpected was occurring. Students had occupied Tiananmen Square to demand democracy. There was no English language paper available, and it was impossible to know what was happening. Was this a great moment of political breakthrough, or was it going to produce appalling repression? No Chinese person would even talk about it, and no Westerner had the faintest idea.

I was in a dilemma. The rainy season was about to begin, and passage across the mountains into the Tibetan region of Muli, one of the three provinces of Kham, would soon become impossible. What was I to do? Tibet itself was under martial law, and now it looked like China too might go the same way. It was impossible to determine the political outcome, so I decided to risk it and go into forbidden territory. I now had to make my way 200 miles to Lugu Lake up on the border of Yunnan, Szechuan, and Muli, from which point I would be able to strike out across the mountains.

The two-day bus journey was rough and muddy across big rivers, steep cliffs, and rain-lashed mountains. When the bus became stuck in mud, all the male passengers had to grab a towrope and haul it out. Eventually we arrived at the lake, a spot of exquisite natural beauty with a small island at its center on which stood the evocative ruins of an old Tibetan monastery. At almost 9,000 feet, this serene body of water perfectly mirrored the sky and clouds above in daylight, while at night intense meteor showers hurtled across the sky.

I could see the mountains of Muli in the distance — a jagged line of peaks way on the Western horizon. I looked in vain for some kind of a guide, but nobody was planning to make that trip until after the rainy season. A Taiwanese man I met translated the opinions of the locals on the advisability of this journey. Don't even think about it, they said; the area is filled with bandits and leopards.

But the weather was beginning to change for the worse, and I could wait no longer. I boarded the rickety daily bus around the lake to Yunming, where the trek would begin. When I arrived, a prolonged torrential downpour began that made any kind of hiking impossible. To my utter surprise, I found myself sharing a room at the local guesthouse with five young Germans who had managed to avoid detection despite their blond hair and strapping builds. As the rain beat down relentlessly in that gray, desolate town, I pondered my rather grim prospects. But then my new friends slowly began to inquire about my intentions. When they learned of the wild trip I planned, they asked eagerly if they could join me. It felt like a stroke of providence, and I agreed with relief. Perhaps they didn't match Rock's armed guard, but one of them was on leave from the German army, another was a triathlete, and all of them were fit and strong.

As we walked out of town the next morning, the tough part really began. We hiked all day toward the mountains through small valleys and it was up, up, up across mountain ridges and into dark forests. At dusk, as we descended exhausted into a new valley from the densely wooded slopes, we came across our first real village, Lichatsu. The inhabitants were stunned at the sight of us, yet after much initial concern and hesitation they proved wonderful hosts, and we were invited to eat in one of the simple wooden houses. The scene inside was like something from the sixteenth century. In the smoky darkness the women all sat to one side, an old granny naked above the waist, and the men cooked us eggs and potatoes in giant black cauldrons hung over a blazing fire.

Early next morning we headed deeper into the mountains. The forests seemed vast, the few trails confusing, the altitude depleting. Eventually we found ourselves on a relatively level plain. In the distance, but much closer than it had appeared from the lake, the strange, jagged ridge of the mountain entrance to the Tibetan world rose above us. That night we camped by a river and ate the last of our food. A tiny older man appeared on the riverbank and genially offered me a pipe of something green that I took to be tobacco, but was never quite sure. My mind raced all night, despite my enormous fatigue, and I slept little if at all.

At dawn a man appeared from nowhere with a string of mules and began to load our packs on them. This was almost too good to be true. It appeared that he would lead us over the pass to Muli and we set off in high spirits with light steps, feeling almost freed from gravity without the weight of our packs. We climbed for hour after hour on a winding track, the forests gradually falling away, sheer rock faces and craggy peaks appearing all around us. But the air was becoming very thin, and despite the lighter loads, it required serious sustained effort to keep going. Suddenly our guide stopped. Had we reached the pass? Was it just 'round the next corner? He indicated that this was as far as he would go and unpacked the animals. Surely we must be close to the top.

It turned out to be another four hours of sheer torture. I staggered on gasping for air, trying to juggle my pack to relieve the cutting shoulder straps, pausing frequently. God knows how high we were. Nobody knew; there were no maps. On we went, past rushing waterfalls, through rain and drizzle, always another bend and another climb just when we thought this had to be the final one.

And then, at last, we reached the top. There was a modest stone wall or "cairn" marking the spot. As we threw ourselves down on the ground in the evening rain, I experienced an enormous thrill. I had made it to the borders of Old Tibet, the fulfillment of a lifelong dream. There were no seven-foot Tibetan border guards of the kind I had read about as a boy, but instead, to my amazement, there indeed was my first herd of yaks grazing two or three hundred yards away, their inscrutable faces barely acknowledging us. The sight of these almost mythic animals suddenly warmed my heart and I felt a huge, exhilarating rush of affirmation.

Now at least it was downhill. As we descended, there were nothing but vast, silent, empty forests and distant mountain ranges. We stumbled as night began to fall, and camped with little if anything to eat and no water. In the morning, far below us, we could make out the shape of a small town down in the valley. After dropping another three or four thousand feet, we began to encounter fields and at last, thankfully, a glimpse of water that looked drinkable, murky though it was. Eventually we reached the river and plunged in, exhausted yet inwardly strong, washing off the days of grime and sweat in the river's cool, rushing waters.

Finally we staggered up the far side of the steep valley to the town. To my disappointment, it appeared to be a settlement with ramshackle buildings and inhabitants mostly in blue and green Mao-style suits. But the people were friendly enough — no Communist commissars, thankfully. However, where was the Tibetan culture? Then I met "the village idiot," a remarkable man. He was unable to speak properly, but his sign language was brilliant. I mentioned the word *gompa*, Tibetan for monastery, and he nodded his head vigorously, pointed into the distance, and beckoned for us to follow him over the rocky bluffs on a small dirt track into another valley, puffs of white cloud high above us. Then, suddenly, there it was! A magnificent Tibetan monastery lay before us. I was stunned. It was covered in wooden scaffolding, and as we approached I could see that it was being built from scratch. Inside, the work was impeccable.

As I looked around, I could see the miserable ruins of the old monastery that must have been destroyed during the Cultural Revolution. And then on a hill above us, I noticed a small temple and a few monks gathered around it in their maroon robes. I ran excitedly to meet them, and they greeted me with amazed but friendly faces. There were about thirty-five monks and before long they had plied us with jasmine tea and a bowl of walnuts and shown us the sacred *thangkas* and prayer wheels of their small home. I was thrilled. Here I was at last in a real live Tibetan monastery, far, far off the beaten path, perhaps the first Westerner to visit. Later, as we left the monks, the late-afternoon sun was setting behind the mountain above them. They stood in a line along the temple wall above us waving silently, emanating a composed and quiet dignity.

Now it was time to head deeper into Kham. I had learned that we were in a town named Wachan where in Joseph Rock's day the Lama King and living Buddha had maintained one of his temple-palaces. We had hiked over a hundred miles in four days and now I was hoping that life would get easier.

Nobody seemed to know anything at all about roads or directions. So I decided to head northwest up a valley that appeared to run deeper into Tibetan territory. We hitched a ride in a pickup truck through a long, narrow valley, and eventually began to climb a winding road to Sanchee, a logging town and one of the most godforsaken spots I have ever encountered anywhere in the world. As we arrived, the locals gaped, and we quickly made our way to the dingy local guesthouse and locked the door. But it was no use. The inhabitants clamored at the dirty window, pressed against the room door, and knocked constantly. If someone opened the door, twenty of them barged in to ask questions. But not about who we were and where we came from. Instead, it was *How much for this pair of boots?* and *What does that watch cost?* The whole town, it seemed, was trying to break down the walls of our room and examine the recesses of our packs.

My young companions had had enough. They had endured agonies of climbing and shared many moments of bewilderment with me. But they were looking for adventure, not to complete some crazed mission for a Tibetan monastery, and they didn't need this kind of intense aggravation. They decided to get out of this dive and hitch back toward Yunnan at first light. My heart sank as I had enjoyed and benefitted from their company, but I couldn't blame them.

By good fortune, a local teenager named Shinkaka emerged from nowhere and told me that there was a pass towards Daocheng, the next town of any size perceptible on my old British map. He volunteered to accompany me on the three-day hike. I couldn't believe my luck. At the earliest opportunity, I left that miserable town and headed once again up into the mountains. Above us were strange, black peaks that looked as if they were made from volcanic ash. We began for the first time to enter the territory of nomads with their black, yak-wool tents scattered along the mountainside. Although this was June, an icy cold began to creep upon us at this high altitude. We pitched my small tent; as night fell, I climbed inside my sleeping bag for warmth.

I was lying there wondering if I was completely mad to be attempting this journey when I heard Shinkaka running toward the tent. He was shouting with great excitement — or was it fear? — "Lurpha! Lurpha!" which was the closest he could get to pronouncing "Ralph." I poked my head out of the tent, and he pointed up into the sky. A full moon had risen above the spiky peaks and I gazed on a still, perfect, star-filled night. I followed the direction of his hand and found myself staring at a coppery, burnished-gold sphere about one-eighth the size of the moon stock-still in the sky, perhaps 5,000 feet above the peaks. What on earth was that?

At first I thought it had to be a balloon, but in the clear moonlight I could see no gondola hanging below it. Shinkaka and I gazed in amazement for fifteen or twenty minutes. During that whole time, it made no movement. What kind of balloon did that? All I could think was that perhaps it was a meteorological balloon, and that tomorrow we would find some kind of weather station on the far side of the pass. It seemed highly unlikely, but what other explanation could there possibly be? I gazed in wonder at this large, perfect, totally stationary sphere. It was not luminous the way science fiction presents such phenomena; it seemed rather to reflect light. Eventually, I was forced back into the tent by the intense cold. I had never had any real interest in UFOs and had never taken speculations about them seriously. But this truly made me wonder.

In the morning, we climbed up to a nomad's tent. Therein the old grandfather lay coughing and dying, wrapped in animal skins beneath an ancient rifle hanging above him. The nomads were friendly and hospitable, offering us *tsampa* barley flour and that horrific-tasting Tibetan tea. I could tell that Shinkaka was asking them about what we had seen as he pointed in the direction of the sphere and spoke excitedly. My Chinese wasn't up to much, but every traveler learns one phrase first, and as they replied to Shinkaka I heard, *"Putong! Putong!"* ("I don't understand, I don't understand!") They said it had appeared in the sky for three nights. From the expressions on their faces, they seemed to regard it as one of life's inscrutable mysteries. Later, as we stumbled across the boulder-strewn, black-rock moonscape at the pass, a sea of mountains emerged before us stretching as far as the eye could see in every direction. Nowhere was there the faintest trace of human activity.

The trail ran high above the tree line at a steady altitude. A wild and ferocious herd of yaks caused us to make a wide detour — those horns looked very sharp, and the beasts had the strength of bison and the agility of horses. Towards midafternoon we met our first human beings since crossing the pass — two men with mules and rifles. It turned out their home village was our destination for the day, and at sunset we descended into a small valley where I saw for the first time the gently tapering stone, square, flat-roofed buildings, each like a mini Potala Palace, that the Khampas build. They hospitably invited us to spend the night camped on the roof of their house. I was carrying twenty-five pictures of the Dalai Lama with me, and it seemed appropriate to give one to each of them. It was clear immediately that I had made friends for life.

Outside the tiny Tibetan village, the riverbanks were strewn with prayer flags, and I felt those wonderful qualities of warmth and generosity that I had glimpsed back at the monastery in Wachan. I slept well that night, and next morning we headed up into the mountains again to cross the second pass. Upon the ridge, the track seemed to go on forever with no sign of habitation and, more worryingly, no water. We pressed on relentlessly, I at least inspired by the great mountain ranges stretching to both

East and West all around us. But the wind was fierce, and the sun at this height burned harshly through the thin air.

Toward late afternoon, we came across a small collection of huts belonging to a group of yak herders. One of them was especially humorous and friendly, and he invited us into his small hut to enjoy *chang* barley beer, yak cheese, and the ever-present tsampa. When I emerged from the hut half an hour later, I heard cries of "Gongga Shan! Gongga Shan!" and saw people pointing to the east. Far in the distance, a magnificent peak in the form of a perfect white pyramid had appeared from amidst the clouds. It was the sacred mountain, a glimpse of which was said to be so rare that it was worth twenty years of meditation. I gazed in wonder at this beautiful sight, which had remained completely cloud-hidden throughout our long trek down the ridge. Gongga Shan had been "discovered" by Joseph Rock in 1931, and for many years was thought to be the highest mountain in the world as, unlike Everest, it rises straight up from the plains below. This glimpse of the perfect crystalline cone of the holy mountain sent shivers down my spine. I was more than glad to take it as a blessing.

I had never seen such a deep valley as the one that now opened up below us. The riverbed had to be 6,000 feet below us, and we trudged on and on, the light fading, down toward our goal: the town of Bezu, where according to Shinkaka I could find lodging, food, and a bus to Daocheng. We arrived at nightfall bone-weary.

But this town was not what I'd expected. The grace and charm of a small Tibetan village were gone. The people were rude and unfriendly, and there was neither shelter nor food available. It is hard to describe what it feels like to arrive exhausted at an unknown town in the heart of the Eastern Himalayas and feel yourself surrounded by hostile people. Again there was that similar quality of intense materialism that I had experienced in the logging town. These Chinese-Tibetan borderlands contained such a mix of attitudes and values. Perhaps it was a romantic streak in me, but it seemed that wherever traditional Tibetan culture remained strong the people had nobility and warmth, and wherever Communist values had taken hold there was little but an intense concern with material possessions.

The following day, I headed alone across the river, looking for the road to Daocheng. But there was only a rough path by the riverside, and there was no alternative but to follow it and hope for the best. I hiked for hours up the valley in the blazing heat. After the high passes it felt dry and scorching, and I saw no trace of vehicle tracks. Soon I began to feel extremely trapped. Ahead of me, the valley seemed to come to a complete dead end as the river appeared to emerge from the foot of a sheer cliff. To each side, steep mountainsides pressed in that I was too tired to climb. And besides, what would be the point? Behind me was a town filled with hostile inhabitants. I felt stuck and lost in a forgotten Himalayan valley in forbidden territory with no way out. A black mood of depression fell on me, and I threw myself down on a rock.

If ever my years of meditation practice came in useful, it was then. I sat, spine erect, on the rock, watching my breath as I tried to center myself. Gradually, breath by breath, the feelings of despair slipped away, and I resolved just to walk on. Within a quarter of a mile, it became clear that the river, in fact, made a sharp ninety-degree turn at what I had thought was the end of the valley. Then two young Tibetan horsemen appeared and told me that yes, I was on the way to Daocheng, but it was seventy kilometers (about forty-five miles) still and many mountains ahead. I felt cheered by the knowledge, and hiked until I could go no farther before asking permission to camp in a dry riverbed in front of a group of traditional stone houses. Playing my ace card again, I pulled out a picture of the Dalai Lama and presented it to a man standing in front of one of the houses. He immediately smiled and gestured that I was welcome to camp here.

What a contrast to the previous night! Children and friendly adults emerged and helped me pitch my tent and light a fire. One man had a small tractor that could pull a cart in which passengers sat, and he agreed to take me the next morning to Daocheng for sixty yuan, perhaps the best four dollars I have ever spent. That night, as a soothing wind rustled through the leaves of the trees above my head, I relaxed for the first time in days.

The next morning my new friend appeared with a tiny tractor hauling a low, wheeled rectangular box in which both I and various Tibetan women sat for the four- or five-hour trip to the nearest town. We climbed up high over another pass, and again the mountains of Kham stretched away to infinity in every direction. Then we began our descent to Daocheng. The town was gray and windswept and a strange mix of Chinese and Tibetan elements. The tractor pulled up in front of the lone guesthouse. There was no one there. And then a young woman appeared. She took one look at me and let out a high-pitched scream. Clearly she had never seen a Westerner before. But after a few minutes, she relented and rented me a bed in the usual dingy communal room. I wondered how I would get from here to Litang, birthplace of the Sixth Dalai Lama, the next stop on my route.

Dusk fell not long after my arrival, and I fell into bed and tried to rest. I was dozing when I was startled by a loud, aggressive knock on the door. I looked at my watch. It was eleven o'clock at night. Bracing myself, I opened the door and found myself gazing at a Chinese policeman in a green uniform, and his Tibetan colleague. The lead cop was extremely hostile, aggressive, and suspicious. My passport was scrutinized thoroughly, but it was clear that no one could read anything except my Chinese visa. Eventually, after an hour of intense shouting of unintelligible questions, they left.

The police were clearly very, very unhappy to see me there, and I expected to be arrested at dawn, as soon as they had communicated with headquarters. Dawn came, however, and nothing happened. Seizing my opportunity, I headed for a forlorn spot on the outskirts of town, where I found a half-derelict set of buildings and a big logging truck. The driver agreed to take me for a small fee and we left, the truck grinding and growling its way through the many low gears needed to move over these forbidding mountains. We were on our way to the second highest town in the world at over 14,000 feet, and we had a load of huge logs.

We picked up speed and rounded a corner; suddenly, there was my first Khampa warrior. He was an elegant and vigorous-looking young man riding a white horse, with his Tibetan cowboy hat, red-braided hair, and a sword. When we got closer, he saw me in the cab and gave me a huge smile as we passed. I was really moved.

We arrived in Litang late at night in icy weather under an enormous, star-filled sky. But there was nowhere to stay. I paced the tiny streets shivering, knocking desperately on doors and receiving no reply. The whole place was boarded up and locked down for the night. Then suddenly a Tibetan man with a warm manner appeared and beckoned me to follow him. He led me into a small guesthouse. We passed first one and then another room full of sleeping Tibetans on small, crude beds. At the back of the house, there was a room near a fire with one narrow bed. He indicated that it was his, but that I should take it. Then he smiled and disappeared. I lay down to rest, relieved and grateful. At last I had arrived in the very world that I had set out to reach a month earlier.

Litang's great monastery in the heart of Kham had a dramatic history in the twentieth century. In the '50s, when the Chinese Communists mounted their surreptitious invasion of eastern Tibet, it had become a focal point of battles between the Khampa guerrillas and the Communist troops. The monastery had been bombed, many monks had been murdered atrociously, and the head lama had been publicly hanged. This was a forgotten piece of history, but for me it was very vivid.

The next morning I bought a Khampa cowboy hat to protect me from the intense sun and cold, and found myself standing next to two of the wildest-looking dudes I have ever seen. With their long, black hair halfway down their backs, their shades, earrings, rakish hats, boots, and swords, they looked like some kind of renegade, half-breed, hippy cowboys. I remembered the Khampa saying I had learned in Dharamsala — "A man without an earring will be reborn as a donkey" — and checked my own turquoise earring that I had been sure to wear.

I tried to keep a low profile in the town, but I knew that eventually the police would arrive. The guesthouse itself was run by a charming older couple. Despite their blue Maoist clothes, they were the soul of Tibetan hospitality, offering me food and tea and inquiring solicitously about my travel plans. Soon the familiar, green-uniformed Chinese policemen arrived with stern faces and ugly demeanors. Where had I come from? Where was I going? When was I leaving Litang and returning to Szechuan? After expressions of helpfulness on my part, they left after securing a promise from me that I would depart the following morning for the four-day journey to Chengdu.

The intensity of my situation now weighed heavily on me. I lay on my simple cot, my solar plexus in a knot. With the tightening surveillance surrounding this more-traveled region, did it make any sense at all to continue? I thought of my girlfriend, Clare, back in Virginia. She had first introduced me to the Nechung Monastery, and I gained some strength from contemplating her love and support. Perhaps wisdom dictated a return to China — after all, it was amazing that I had made it this far, and I already had memories to last a lifetime. I walked up a hillside and sat in the piercing sunlight as I tried to compose my thoughts and priorities. I gazed long and hard over that high valley, turning over all the options, looking for inspiration. The more I thought about it, the more I felt that having come this far, it made no sense to turn back before I had achieved my objective. Despite the stress and anxiety, and with considerable trepidation, I resolved to go on.

I informed my gracious hosts in the guesthouse that I would be leaving for Szechuan at five in the morning. Delightful and caring as ever, they got up with me in the bitter cold, and boiled water for me to take on my trip. I said my slightly guilty goodbyes, headed out of the door into the icy, pitch-black night, and gazed out on the broad valley with its enormous dome of crystal stars. My plan was to walk west through the town and hike several miles up the mountain, where I would conceal myself until the first vehicles began their journey in the morning deeper into Tibetan territory. Then I would try to hitch a ride.

I walked alone through the silent, freezing town, the only sound the eerie echoes of my own footsteps. There was only one small light in the center of town, and I was concerned that a barking dog might awaken the people inside, who I suspected to be police. I tried to tiptoe around this isolated lamp, my heart in my mouth, and my spirits lifted when I passed it without incident. I clamped my Khampa hat more firmly down on my head to ward off the night cold, and strode into the hills. By first light, Litang had become a distant sight down in the valley, and I wrapped myself in my sleeping bag and hid behind a stone wall to await the first trucks. The first two vehicles ignored me, but the third, a pickup driven by two young Chinese men, pulled up. I offered them the familiar few dollars, threw my pack in the back, and climbed in the cab with a rush of exhilaration. Thank God.

They drove like maniacs, leaving a high dust plume behind them in the thin air. On we went in the early-morning sunlight. Suddenly, they stopped in a great silent valley where a small dirt road led off at right angles. I got out and watched their dust plume disappear in the distance. The sun had not yet risen over the tops of the mountains, and down in the valley was a tranquil, deserted turquoise lake. It was in the most remote place I had ever been dropped in all my years of hitchhiking, but I felt free and happy.

There was no choice but simply to walk on. I put on my pack and, with a quiet inner joy despite the vast empty silence around me, started walking deeper into Tibet. I hadn't gone far when I saw a group of mounted nomads slowly driving their yaks towards the lake. They crossed the road just fifty feet ahead of me. A beautiful Tibetan girl of about seventeen with long hair braided with turquoise and coral and wearing high boots rode slowly past me on a white horse. A little way in the distance, her father and brothers, rifles slung across their backs, moved gracefully in their saddles. As I gazed at this vision of feminine beauty, she seemed to me like a symbol of the old Tibet: proud, free, untouched by the horrors of materialism. I stood silently by the roadside and felt a deep reverence for the fading beauties of traditional Tibetan culture.

Then they were gone, and I walked on down the valley. Before long I was able to flag a ride farther west toward my destination. As the truck rumbled past still, aquamarine lakes set like precious stones below high, snowcapped mountain peaks, I noticed pilgrims making their way to Lhasa prostration by prostration, their knees protected by leather pads, their clothes ragged and torn, their faces weather-beaten, their spirits undaunted and invincible. In the distance, set right in the heart of the valley, my eye fell on a large *stupa*, a place of deep sanctity around which pilgrims had gathered. I was coming home to sacred Tibet.

I would like to describe more fully what followed, but for the protection of all involved, it is impossible. After my final ride I lay beside a rushing river, half hidden by an old stone bridge, wondering how to complete my journey. With a mind filled with dark thoughts, I could see no way to make the connections I needed in this remote spot. Then children began to gather 'round me to play, and my spirits lifted. After a couple of hours, a Tibetan man approached me and beckoned mysteriously to follow him through a maze of tiny village alleys. He disappeared suddenly through a hole in a long wall, and I followed him. To my amazement, I stepped into the center of a small but ancient monastery where I was able to hand on the material I had carried. I was assured that traders left every two weeks for the heart of Tibet, and that they would carry this precious cargo to its final destination. It seemed that I had achieved my objective; it was an immense relief.

Now I had to get back to China without detection. It was a bumpy, crowded, and smoke-filled bus ride of endlessly dusty days winding across arid mountainsides. After a number of close scrapes, I arrived in Kangding, which Mao himself in his memoirs describes as the border of Tibet. As the rickety old bus gradually descended the winding road toward the town, I was struck by the exceptional ugliness of the place. Every building seemed poorly constructed and devoid of charm, with virtually the whole town built in an ungainly sprawl. But as we neared the town center below us, I could see one magnificent building at its heart, surrounded on all sides by a warren of narrow streets. I wondered what it was, and expected never to know the answer.

As we pulled up at the bus station, the driver announced completely unexpectedly that we would stop for four hours at this curious place. *Well,* I thought, *this is my last stop in Tibetan culture, and I'm going to try to find that building.* I guessed roughly where it might be, and threaded my way toward it.

I turned a corner in a maze of back alleys and suddenly there it was — an exquisite monastery combining perfectly the pagoda-like architecture of China with the vivid colors and forms of Tibet. As I approached, three monks appeared and invited me in. Within the courtyard there was a huge door that I took to be the entrance to the temple. Would I like to enter? As the monk swung open the doors, a thirty-foot gilded statue of the Buddha appeared with twenty-foot Bodhisattvas seated on each side. Realizing these would be my last moments among Tibetan spiritual imagery, not knowing what news awaited me of political turmoil back in China, I decided to do a final meditation, expressing gratitude for my safe emergence from a month in forbidden territory. I closed my eyes in silent contemplation and reverence and gave thanks for all those forces, seen and unseen, which had enabled me to complete this journey.

Opening my eyes after fifteen minutes, I stood to leave. As I did so, my gaze fell on a striking statue just to the right of a Bodhisattva. Where had I seen this fierce figure before? Then it suddenly dawned on me. Turning to the monk who had greeted me, I asked, "Nechung Chogyam?" He nodded vigorously. It was indeed none other than the Nechung protector whose image I had last seen in Dharamsala months earlier when the senior monk of the Nechung Monastery had promised that he would put me under the deity's protection for the duration of this task. Perhaps it was simply synchronicity, but I was in no mood for such speculation. To me it felt like a blessing, and I was flooded with profound feelings. There could be no sweeter conclusion to my hike on the wild eastern side of Tibet, and as I headed back to that dingy bus station, my heart was singing.

★ ★ ★ ★ ★

When I eventually returned to China proper, I gazed with horror on the first television screen I had seen in over a month. The news was filled with secret surveillance shots of student leaders doing something incriminating like holding up a V FOR VICTORY sign during the long demonstrations in Tiananmen Square. Then they were shown being dragged out of police vans, hair tousled, eyes wild, clearly frightened after a night in the cells. Viewers were left with an image of their interrogation by hard-faced, uniformed police officers.

So the worst-case scenario had occurred after all, I realized. My heart sank when I thought of the suffering and the lost opportunity. What exactly had happened? In the center of Chengdu, about twenty-five burned-out fire trucks and buses had been gathered around the familiar concrete statue of the Great Helmsman. The windows of Communist Party Headquarters had been smashed, and part of a city block appeared to have been devastated by fire. But, apart from that, things appeared relatively normal. The power of the Party was everywhere. When it chose to use its overwhelming power, nothing could challenge its grip.

I picked up the *China Daily*, the country's English-language paper, and read of the "counterrevolutionary rebels" who, aided by foreign-intelligence services, had tried to overthrow the State. These tools of bourgeois forces had forgotten the primacy of class warfare, and needed re-schooling in the objective, scientific principles of Marxist-Leninist Mao Tse-tung thought, wherein pride of place was given to that absurd oxymoron, the "People's Democratic Dictatorship." I felt the dead hand of extreme materialism close around China's heart like a fist with rigor mortis.

My small gesture of support for freedom in Tibet was, of course, minuscule compared with this. But I was glad that I had made it. If nothing else, it was a kind of initiation in courage for me, and an expression of faith in the ultimate triumph of the human spirit. When my plane took off from Kunming, I knew the mountains of Kham would always hold a special place in my psyche. As we rose through the clouds and my last glimpse of China faded, I felt more deeply than ever that the greatest truths about the human condition could never be approached without an awakening to spiritual insight. Without this, life is an empty struggle. For me, Tibet will always stand as the supreme symbol of collective dedication to the esoteric truths without which we stumble on in a desert of materialism. My time in eastern Tibet only served to strengthen my dedication to this ultimate liberation without which we are, in Goethe's words, "Only a troubled guest on the dark earth."

∞

CHAPTER TEN

AWAKENING EASTERN EUROPE AND RUSSIA

In the autumn of 1989, as I returned from my journey around the world, global politics were changing. Mikhail Gorbachev was leading changes in Soviet and world politics toward greater sanity. But few dared hope that the ramshackle edifice of Communism would come crashing down as quickly as it did.

When my girlfriend Clare, with whom I was living half the week in Alexandria, Virginia, called to inform me that the Berlin Wall was coming down, it confirmed my conviction to go to Eastern Europe. My travels had long ago convinced me that most citizens of the planet share a common human decency and have similar hopes and dreams of happiness and fulfillment. They also share a yearning for insight into the truths that make the riddles of life intelligible. This relatively unknown part of the planet would be a good test of my conviction of the universality of this awakening. Eastern Europe felt like something out of a time warp. Inside the ornate restaurants of Budapest, traces of the Austro-Hungarian Empire were everywhere. Pillars of polished marble surrounded gypsy orchestras while waiters dressed from the 1930s offered menus of sophistication and minimal cost. On the battlements of the old city of Buda were heroic statues of medieval kings who had fought the Turks and considered themselves the Eastern bulwark of Christendom. This was a mythology of which I was almost totally ignorant.

Politically, those early years after the demise of Communism offered a tiny window of opportunity for alternative, holistic, and green thinkers. For the first year, it seemed that those dissidents possessing the moral courage to challenge totalitarianism were actually nearing levels of power. These were remarkably open-minded people, sympathetic to the non-materialistic values of Western counterculture. One day in the early '90s, I walked into the office of the Ministry of Culture in Warsaw and was shocked to see the latest Open Center catalogue on the junior minister's desk. But it was not long before conservative parties began to use the marketing techniques of Madison Avenue to put people in power who would privatize the economy and sell it off to multinational corporate bidders. The courageous former dissidents were fascinated by alternatives to consumer capitalism but, unfortunately, their time was short.

I first visited Prague in 1991, and the city exuded magic. Not a single advertisement or neon sign was visible, and a deep silence fell after dark. The Hradčany Palace, with its ancient cathedral, rose above Malá Strana and conveyed a sense of mysterious beauty and harmony. Everywhere towers and spires evoked a dim collective memory of a time filled with occult wisdom and alchemy. You could stumble into a wine bar on a winding lane in the Old Town and drink inconspicuously with Czechs in a city drenched with soul. A year later, this had become a memory.

My first trip to Poland involved a nightlong ride in a creaky, dim, mostly empty train chugging painfully though the Tatra Mountains to a world of total grayness. In Krakow the streets were gray, the faces of the people were gray, the sky was gray, and a bone-chilling wind swept through the desolate streets. That same inhuman repression of individuality that was so evident in post-Mao China was everywhere apparent in Poland, and only served to deepen my horror of any political system based on a purely materialistic view of history and human motivation.

There was still something forbidding for a Westerner arriving in Moscow at the beginning of the '90s. After a lifetime of seeing the Russians presented as our sworn enemies, the mere sight of soldiers with fur hats, jackboots, and Kalashnikovs was enough to generate a few tremors as I approached customs and immigration. But it was the gritty intensity of Moscow that impressed me most. I was disturbed to see massive, polluting power plants in the center of Moscow, and to realize that almost everyone lived in huge, anonymous high rises like some vast, citywide federal housing project. But once I had entered these homes, I found that identikit apartments could be made into homes as individualized and cozy as log cabins in the woods. Add to this the way in which Russians have preserved the old spirit of hospitality, of treating every visitor as an honored guest, and I developed more feeling for the Russian heart. Everywhere I went, I was greeted with warmth and deep fascination with the work I was doing back in the States.

An ancient mystical spirit dwelt in the Russian soul, and there was a yearning for the spiritual truths that Communism had denied. People were eager to acquaint themselves with the teachings now so widely available in the States and Europe. And Russia itself had esoteric and healing traditions dating back centuries about which many Russians at that time had only a dim inkling.

I knew about Gurdjieff and Ouspensky and their circles in St. Petersburg before the First World War. I had a dim sense of the Silver Poets, and the lost years between the beginning of the twentieth century and the Bolshevik Revolution. I had been touched by the beauty of *The Way of a Pilgrim*, the Russian Orthodox classic on the mystical practice of continuous prayer centered in the heart, and was vaguely aware of the widespread monasteries that seemed to have maintained a deep if obscure spirituality through the centuries of Russian suffering and survival.

But nothing prepared me for the flirtatiousness of Russian women. After decades in which the homely wives of Khrushchev and Brezhnev had been our only images of Russian females, it was a shock to realize that so many of them were beautiful, and that they dressed in the most stylish way, especially given their very limited resources. The next shock was realizing that they were almost all married. In Russia, everyone was married by their early twenties, as it was the only way to find an apartment away from parents. By the time people were in their late twenties or thirties, many were having affairs. It appeared that sex was the one great pleasure that Big Brother allowed the masses, apart from cheap vodka and cigarettes.

In St. Petersburg, I found myself on television being interviewed about the relationship between men and women. When I suggested that an egalitarian relationship between the sexes was actually more fun and more creative than the old macho dominance, I faced blank and uncomprehending stares from the male TV crew. The women themselves clearly thought differently, as I learned when three women simultaneously kissed me after a talk in which I had suggested that the old forms of male dominance were bound to go the same way as the dinosaurs.

Those early visits to Russia had a poignancy and sweetness that is probably impossible to find today. There is a peculiar intensity when people come together on a human level after a lifetime of having seen each other as the great enemy. At the conclusion of a workshop in a workers' vacation center outside Moscow in which we'd tried to give ideas how to start and develop holistic centers to sixty participants from throughout the former Soviet Union, from the Baltics to Kazakhstan, two people stood to read poems they had written about their learning experiences. Someone else suggested that we had talked and listened together, but there was one thing we had not done with our voices: sing. She began a beautiful Russian folksong, and every person in the room joined this expression of gratitude. There was such an ancient depth of feeling in that song, so much soul and longing in that melody, that there was barely a dry eye in the house. It was as if the very heart of Russia opened to thank us for bringing some genuine spirit following eighty years of dead ideology.

Of course, it was the lack of consumer culture in Russia that had kept the old folksongs so alive. Russian gypsy music exuded soul, and Russians retained a wonderful instinct for melody and emotional depth. One of the pleasures in the aftermath of Communism was the sound of melodious oldies from the West unexpectedly blasting from taxi radios in the most startling places. As we rounded an impressive statue of Lenin in the city of his name, suddenly the old Searchers hit "Needles and Pins" filled the car. How the aching human heart finds expression even in the most life-denying political context.

Everywhere in Eastern Europe you would find yourself hearing old B-sides from the Beatles, some of the best songs they ever wrote, half-forgotten in the West but preserved in the Communist world as authentic and beautiful. Sitting in the barely furnished restaurant of a small hotel in Třeboň, yards from the castle that preserved the records of John Dee's enigmatic sojourn in Bohemia, feeling far, far away from Western culture and the English language, suddenly the minor chords and poignant harmonies of the early Beatles — with all their tender post-Hamburg feelings of loss — rang out from a tinny radio in the corner. I hadn't heard that song in years. Little did I know at the time of the gorgeous feeling for music that permeates Bohemia, and the sublime skills of its singers and musicians.

My connection with Russia had begun when I was on holiday in South Wales at the age of eleven and saw Eisenstein's film, *Alexander Nevsky*. The noble prince's defense of Novgorod against the insidious power of the Teutonic Knights had stirred me in some inexplicable way. So it was a big surprise when on my first visit to Russia I found myself standing beneath the great statue of the Prince of Novgorod, erected to celebrate a thousand years of Christianity in Russia, surrounded by the red brick walls of the city enclosing medieval watchtowers, whitewashed walls, and the golden domes of the Cathedral of St. Sophia. *What kind of synchronicity was this?* I wondered as I gazed up at Alexander's resolute face.

In Warsaw, I heard the Norwegian philosopher of deep ecology, Arne Næss, speak at a small center I had helped to emerge. He drew a triangle on the blackboard with each of the three points marked in red, blue, and green. It was his contention that Poland needed to move from red Communist state to green eco-society, but that almost certainly it would be moved first by powerful forces into the blue world of corporate capitalism. Eastern Europe, it seemed, would have to make the same mistakes that we had in the West before people tired of wrecked environments, exhausting work hours, the primacy of money, and the replacement of political oppression with wage slavery. My Polish friend Przemko, after a few years of Western-style capitalism, recalled wistfully the days in Poland when it was still possible to have a serious conversation that did not revolve around questions of money.

As for me, I found the egalitarianism of the post-Communist world pretty acceptable. I didn't mind that almost everyone had a similar income level and lived in homes of comparable modesty. At least everyone had a country *dacha,* no matter how small, and the mental stress produced by an urban America cut off from all rural contact was mostly avoided. Despite the political oppression, there had been a place for culture in a socialist state. People may not have had money and freedom, but they did have time. Something dignified of old European culture had been preserved among artists and intellectuals. Strolling in the evening through old-town Warsaw, my friends would greet fellow thinkers with warmth and charm. For all its grimness, the dreary world of Communist Eastern Europe had still maintained something special, whether it was the silence and beauty of old Prague or the artistic culture of Poland.

Who cannot be moved by the depth of suffering endured by Poland in the twentieth century, and the dogged endurance of its people against unbearable sorrow and oppression? Here was the site of the Warsaw Ghetto, there a place that boy scouts engaged in a shootout with the Gestapo to free resistance fighters on their way to Auschwitz, further down the street was a spot where gardeners protected Jews in a hidden cellar until both fugitives and protectors were discovered and murdered. Trapped between Hitler and Stalin, doomed to decades of totalitarianism, the spirit of the Polish people never broke — although the universal grayness that had greeted me in Krakow on my first visit showed how desperate it had become.

I'm glad I made a small contribution to the shift away from the totalitarian nightmare of the early '90s. I used to fly into Moscow in the dead of winter carrying a money belt containing donations by sympathetic foundations to support fledgling holistic initiatives. One evening at the end of a winter workshop held on the grounds of Sukhanova, an eighteenth-century mansion outside Moscow, I found myself tramping through the snow with my new Russian friends. As we marched through the birch forest, the snow fell thickly and a sense of warm camaraderie enveloped the group. When we reached the tiny, rusting train station and boarded a ramshackle carriage to carry us back to the city, the group burst forth into traditional Russian songs that could have been sung by soldiers on their way to the Nazi front fifty years earlier. As I listened to their soulful strains, I pondered the course my life had taken. When I had taken those first, tentative steps on the spiritual path in the deserts of New Mexico a quarter century earlier, I could never have imagined that the path would lead me to this — the fur hats, the smiling Slavic features, the drunks on the train joining in the songs, the sense that this remote world could offer such a gracious welcome and that I could so easily feel myself a part of it.

I had fallen in love with Russian soulfulness, the indomitable spirit of Poland, and the beauty and mystery of the Czech Republic. As my attention turned back to New York in the mid-'90s and another phase of my life came to a close, I looked back on my experiences in the post-Communist world with immense gratitude. I felt enriched by my contact with these cultures. I had experienced the good fortune of actually finding those spiritual brothers and sisters whose existence behind the former Iron Curtain I had intuited when the Berlin Wall fell.

I had also become aware of half-forgotten esoteric traditions, brilliant moments in the history of consciousness, that had been lost not only to us in the West but also to most people in Eastern Europe itself. Now perhaps I could play a role in returning to them the attention they deserved. The alchemists of Renaissance Bohemia for one deserved our appreciation as integral parts of a spiritual lineage in Europe that only now could we piece together fully.

And when I departed Russia with a heavy heart, I was grateful for a hundred outrageous experiences that would always leave me with a glow of warmth: memories of vodka and champagne, parties, workshops, and friends. They stay with me always, and bring a glint of joy to my heart whenever I turn my inner gaze towards the East.

∞

CHAPTER ELEVEN

THE GLOBAL NETWORK
OF HOLISTIC CENTERS

AN ECOLOGY OF CONSCIOUSNESS,
WEST COAST STYLE

For thirty years I have had the good fortune to be involved in a growing global network of centers, an ecology of consciousness becoming aware of itself that spans the planet. When we meet, we do so in a spirit of openness, mutual support, friendship, and love. We are autonomous initiatives within our own cultures, but we also recognize that we are facets of a greater diamond of expanding consciousness.

I have come to know centers throughout North America from British Columbia to Big Sur, California; from San Francisco to New York — also in Europe from Spain to Russia and from Scotland to Italy. Many more flourish in Australia, New Zealand, Brazil, South Africa, and other parts of the Southern Hemisphere. Today people are creating centers in Vietnam, Laos, Kenya, India, and even China.

Attending these Gatherings has been one of the delights of my life. Not only have many friendships formed, but these events have often led mysteriously to fresh openings of destiny. We can live with a broad if somewhat diffuse conviction that a more holistic approach to life is truly developing throughout the planet, but these Gatherings give it form, substance, and specificity. They have warmed my heart and strengthened my convictions around the growing influence of beneficent and life-enhancing powers in the world. Here are some glimpses of these focal points for the emergence of a new culture.

Driving down Route 1 in California south of the Monterey Bay, I entered the enchanted world of Big Sur, much beloved by Henry Miller after his sojourn in Paris. Mountains sweep down to the Pacific Ocean; the road winds around headlands, over bridges, always framing the shining, crashing sea below, with its long streams of spray and spume sweeping in waves to the rugged shore, the bright sunlight glinting off the waves into 10,000 ever-shifting, flashing shards.

I first had a small taste of Esalen Institute at the heart of Big Sur in the mid-'70s after returning from Colombia. Then my friends and I had driven down from Berkeley with little money and the intention to spend the night in the legendary hot tubs.

Back in 1962, the same year as the founding of Findhorn, Michael Murphy and Dick Price, graduate students at Stanford University, established Esalen Institute on the site of hot springs used for millennia by the Esalen Indians, twenty-one acres of beauty pervaded by the constant rhythm of the crashing ocean. To this day, to sit naked in the hot tubs, listening to the waves below and gazing at the star-filled sky, is to enjoy a quintessential experience of the human-potential movement.

It was at a pioneering retreat center named Rancho La Puerta in Baja California, Mexico that Michael Murphy met Aldous Huxley in the late '50s. Huxley encouraged him to start a center for the exploration of new ideas about consciousness, psychology, perennial philosophy, and the new practices necessary to turn away from the looming prospect of a Brave New World. How appropriate that the writer of one of the two great dystopian novels of the twentieth century should play an inspirational role in seeding one of the seminal institutions underscoring the explosion of consciousness of the '60s.

But it was another expatriate Brit, Alan Watts, who taught the first seminar at Esalen. Nobody at that time made Buddhism and Eastern spiritual teachings more accessible to the West than him, doing so in his debonair, nonsectarian, joyous way. Then came the psychologist Abraham Maslow and his pioneering work on the hierarchy of human needs, self-actualization, and peak experiences. Fritz Perls and Gestalt psychology followed, and Dick Price, Esalen's cofounder, became his leading student. The emotional candor and intimacy, the clearing of blocks and angers, became the core practice at Esalen. This must surely have been crucial in ensuring that fifty years later Esalen continues to flourish, showing no sign of losing its enduring appeal.

When I visited Esalen for the Centers' Gathering, I immediately felt that this gorgeous spot was continuing to serve a beautiful purpose. It was teaching people ways to connect with their authentic selves, and reach out to others in a spirit of warmth and service as independent beings free to express themselves without dogma or inhibition.

Whenever I spend time at Esalen, I experience it as one of the heavenly realms on this earth. The steady, soothing crashing of the ocean below; the comfort with nudity; the vibrant, multi-hued gardens and organic farm; the commitment to sustainability and emotional honesty; and the ongoing range of programs concerned with personal and social transformation — all of this maintains Esalen's position as a brilliant achievement, an engine for new ideas, and a place where the commitment continues to wholeness, living in the moment, and creating a healthy future for humanity.

Breitenbush Hot Springs in the Cascade Mountains of Oregon is the only worker-owned cooperative I know among the centers, and a place totally off the grid. It heats itself in the snowy winters with geothermal energy from pipes that run deep underground, and generates electricity with hydropower from the multiple cascading falls around the property. This thirty-five-year-old experiment in radical democracy and ecology flourishes with more vigor than ever today.

Peter Moore, Breitenbush's business director, exudes the rough and ready charm of a man who signed up thirty-five years ago, after four years in Europe and India, to convert a broken-down old spa resort into an alternative community. Working without pay in the early years, delivering his first child in the snowy darkness without electricity, heat, or midwife, Peter captures that progressive Oregonian tradition — can do, ready for anything, undeterred by obstacles, willing to get one's hands dirty, and committed to doing things differently, democratically, and cooperatively despite the arduous nature of this path.

Tom Robinson, the program and marketing director, brings the suave air of a man well versed in business practices in his earlier life but also psychologically sophisticated, calm, and deeply attuned to group process. When I met Tom, I knew I had an ally committed to the continuity of the Centers' Gathering, someone who saw its value and was fully present and organizationally adroit.

It will come as no surprise that the West Coast of both America and Canada is home to the greatest concentration of centers on the planet. One of my favorites is the Mount Madonna Center in the Santa Cruz Mountains above Monterey Bay. Its spiritual inspiration was Baba Hari Dass, a Hindu spiritual teacher who appeared in Ram Dass' *Be Here Now* in which he found his guru in a remote ashram. Baba Hari Dass had taken a vow of silence before Ram Dass encountered him in the ashram. He was skilled at creating mountain ashrams, and came quietly to America before *Be Here Now* was published. Such a vow precludes celebrity, and he maintained a low profile, gathering students in the San Francisco Bay Area and eventually buying an old apple farm in the late '70s on a mountain ridge, where he started a community and learning center from very modest beginnings.

Mount Madonna is rare among holistic centers in that it has a living teacher from India. The members of the community are creative, and possessed of an independent spirit. Brajesh, the program director, has lived a life emblematic of the way a deeper calling interrupts an academic career. He is the only person I know who went from receiving his PhD in political science from Harvard to working as a Volkswagen mechanic in an alternative community in the Ozarks, and then to finding his way to Mount Madonna.

Each time I visit Mount Madonna, I experience a sweet taste of eternity. As the rays of the early-morning sun stream through the redwood trees, a layer of clouds lies below and the air is sweet with pine resin and with silence. The soothing tinkling of one of many waterfalls eases my heart and calms my solar plexus from the rush of New York. The haunting sound of a conch blown at sunrise offers blessings in the Hanuman Temple, the abode of the Hindu monkey god, liberator from obstacles. As the sun rises and the clouds disperse, my gaze turns to the Monterey Bay coastline far below and the fruit-filled valley beneath with its strawberries, blueberries, artichokes, and hardworking Mexican agricultural laborers who play an unsung, demanding role in bringing America's fruit to market, as I know well from my own time working in the apple and pear orchards of the Hood River Valley.

Once again, like Breitenbush, like Findhorn, like Omega and many other centers, Mount Madonna has risen from the most modest and uncertain beginnings. Through commitment to the power of community, to a contemporary mystical spirituality and to service to humanity, a fresh force has appeared in the world. How many thousands of participants have sat in silence in Mount Madonna's impeccably clean, open, and fresh meditation hall to imbibe the wisdom of yoga, or to take one of the many workshops in creativity, poetry, mythology, or psychology? Once again, a twenty-first-century ashram, an alert, freethinking community devoted to a higher good, a tranquility for the confused, and a transcendent experience of beauty to many. For the lucky few, it has even opened the door to a taste of eternity. For this, no words of gratitude are enough.

One of the places that has become a true soul home is Cortes Island, one of the Gulf Islands of British Columbia. Located almost a thousand miles north of Esalen, protected from the ocean storms by the mountainous length of Vancouver Island to the west, these islands gaze out on the snow-covered, jagged peaks of the Coastal Range to the east, exuding calm and beauty.

I stand on a deserted, rocky beach on Cortes Island; silence fills the air; a large blackbird flies directly overhead at treetop height, the flap, flap of its wingbeat the only sound to complement the lap of the ocean passageway. To stand by the water in the early morning is to have not only one's own beach, but one's own ecosystem. The sun rises above the peaks to the east; the wind soughs through the branches of alder, pine, and cedar as I gaze in serenity, touched by the spirit of the great North; the forested mountains stretch to Alaska, and the turbulence of America lies beyond the horizon to the south.

Cortes Island, named after the Spanish captain who first sighted it in the eighteenth century, is home to Hollyhock,

Canada's leading center for holistic learning and personal renewal. Located on the southern end of the island, reachable by two ferries from the logging town of Campbell River on Vancouver Island, this is about as far north as it's possible to go on the West Coast before issues of accessibility and climate arise. If the New York Open Center is the ultimate urban center, Hollyhock is the ultimate wilderness center.

Before there was Hollyhock, there was the Cold Mountain Institute, founded in 1969, the year a ferry began to run to the island, by Gestalt psychologists inspired by Esalen. Those who experienced the three-month resident-fellows program at Cold Mountain emerged as fundamentally different human beings after extended group processes in the wilderness in which fears, blocks, fantasies, truths, and lies were explored in a setting where freedom and honesty could prevail uninterruptedly. Say what you mean; mean what you say; and come from the heart.

Cold Mountain closed after about a dozen years following the death of one of its founders. But the buildings remained standing, and a few years later one of the original members of Greenpeace, Rex Weyler, persuaded his mother to loan him and a group of friends a small sum sufficient to put on a summer program of holistic events. They named the new center Hollyhock because that was the flower blooming in abundance amongst the empty buildings when the idea had first come to create the center.

Blessed by serene beauty and soaring eagles, the beaches are covered in oysters ripe for the shelling. With the island's mix of First Nations, descendants of fishermen and apple farmers, and old and new pioneers committed to organic food and sustainable practice, Cortes is a natural home for experiments in evolving a new culture. Far enough to feel distant from the stresses of contemporary life but not too remote to feel isolated, Cortes to me represents a gift of peace. A visit there is always sublime.

My close friend Philip Wood, another expatriate Brit, who came to Canada as a twenty-one-year-old escaping Blackpool and Derby, served as Hollyhock's board chair in the early years. We met at the Centers' Gatherings at Omega and Esalen back in the 1980s when only a handful of centers attended. Cortes has now been an integral part of my life for over twenty years, a necessary balance to the concrete and noise of New York.

Looking west across the Pacific Ocean to Hawaii's Big Island we find yet another hub of holistic awareness, Kalani Honua. When I first arrived there, I saw lush tropical trees meeting overhead to form a welcoming archway. The black lava fields from the Haleakala volcano steam into the ocean just a few miles away, and the welcoming spirit of Aloha permeates the atmosphere. Started by dancer Richard Koob on a stretch of property owned by his family, Kalani today has evolved into perhaps the largest of the Hawaiian holistic centers, with a strong relationship with the local indigenous Hawaiian community, and is valued for its economic contribution to one of the poorer sections of the archipelago. There is a gracious ease to life on the Big Island, a feeling for the spirit of the great ocean that surrounds this remote archipelago. At Kalani, and other Hawaiian centers, a veneration for the ancient Hawaiian ways, with all their wisdom and beauty, lies close to the surface.

A little farther down the coast, I stand on the black-sand beach a few kilometers from Kalani, the aroma of cannabis drifting through the salty air, naked men and women beating conga drums or playing other instruments, the warm ocean sighing rhythmically. On this part of the island, the sun is rarely relentless and unforgiving. Instead, a veil of mist frequently obscures the sun for a few minutes while the temperature remains perfect, the moist, windy climate a delight. This is a place where the soul is soothed, the heart finds peace, and the spirit is uplifted by the constant presence of beauty.

Most centers, like Kalani and Hollyhock, do not associate themselves directly with a single spiritual tradition. The multiple paths to inner development and personal growth — the dance, music, song, and poetry from all world cultures — together form the heart of the holistic approach. Today, all centers worth their salt are working toward sustainability, incorporating every green building, living machine, and wind or hydro generator possible. For the holistic and the ecological are simply two sides of the same coin. Our personal transformation serves little if it is unaccompanied by a positive social and environmental direction.

With today's relentless media, one never has to wait long for stories of horror and corruption that can generate feelings of hopelessness and cynicism. But there is a subtle counterforce in the world today. It may be small numerically, but it is spreading, and it is attuned to a healthy and sustainable direction for all of us. These modest holistic centers may only serve a tiny percentage of the overall population, but they are powerhouses of positive change.

This is cultural evolution, not political revolution. Change is gradual, but increasingly pervasive. I no longer stop with a tingling thrill when I see the word "holistic" in the *New York Times*. Now it seems the *Times* barely publishes two successive editions without some kind of reference to this subtle transformation. The glamorous yogini in the Hamptons; the rise of wind and solar power; the questioning of economic growth as the only measure of progress; the growing emphasis on national well-being; the scientifically validated cognitive benefits of meditation — the list is becoming endless.

Twenty-five years ago, these centers of holistic learning were just fledgling initiatives pulled together on a wing and a prayer, drawing on the youthful idealism of their staffs, hoping to survive another year and accustomed to the skepticism of the mainstream media. When I look back on those months in Vancouver in 1971 taking my first tentative steps on the spiritual path and selling ecology magazines door to door, and I compare that experience to the plethora of holistic centers, meditation retreats, and ecovillages that exist today, I can only feel grateful deep down in my soul for this evolution. Someone like me in 1971 setting out to explore ideas and writers outside the academic and cultural mainstream no longer needs to walk a lonely and frightening path. We have a vibrant if diffuse holistic culture now on a worldwide basis.

From the humblest beginnings, from windswept trailer parks, from remote hot springs, from abandoned summer camps and old apple farms, an alternative network is rising that feeds the soul of modern human beings. It's a story that has passed largely unnoticed beneath the radar of the media. But this movement is strong, and draws its nourishment from the waters of life itself and from the endurance of humanity's mystical traditions. It seeps with the force of a rising tide into the nooks and crannies of a dried-out world. It brings joy to the hearts of the many who taste it, and carries the future within its noble heart.

PART THREE

ON THE JEWELED
HIGHWAY

CHAPTER TWELVE

∞

MEETING THE MAN
ON HAʻENA BEACH

RUDOLF STEINER AND THE
RETURN OF THE MYSTERIES

As for my own spiritual journey, I needed to travel far to the
West to find a true philosopher, a lover of wisdom who spoke
not only to my intellect but also to my heart and to my impulse
to create positive change in the world. By the spring of 1985,
shortly after the first year of the Open Center and my thirty-sixth
birthday, I was exhausted. I had poured my lifeblood into the
creation of the Open Center, and my body and soul were badly
in need of refreshment and renewal. When my friend Sam, the
whitewater rafter, suggested that I head for the Na Pali Coastline
trail on the island of Kauaʻi, the most westerly of the Hawaiian
Islands, it felt like the perfect move.

After the rush of stress of New York City, I longed for silence,
space, and serenity. As my plane took off from Oakland Airport,
banked, and headed over the Golden Gate Bridge and out across
the great Pacific Ocean, I looked down on the scudding traces of
cloud below me and felt a rush of sheer exhilaration. Freedom,
the endless expanse of water, the sense of heading somewhere no
one I knew well had ever gone before.

Arriving on Kauaʻi, I hitchhiked to the start of the trail.
For eleven miles, the tiny path clung to steep, otherworldly

mountainsides as they plunged down to the turquoise Pacific. For a week I alternated between fatigue and bliss, as the steady rhythm of the infinite ocean lulled my tired brain to rest, and the sparkling sunlight flashed off the waves below, sending surges of exhilaration up my spine.

By the time I returned to Ha'ena Beach at the start of the trail, I was calm and filled with the right kind of emptiness. A week of jagged emerald ridges, groves of ripe mangoes, and uninterrupted blue horizons smoothed the stress from New York and left me receptive and open.

One afternoon, as a giant gray cloud slid slowly across the sky, it began to rain softly. I retreated into my tent and opened the first of the books I had brought with me. As the waves crashed along the shore and the rain pattered down on the tent, I slipped into the sleeping bag I had bought in New York just a couple of days before my departure. What better place to read a book called *The Tension Between East and West* than Hawaii? I read the first two pages and my attention quickened. Suddenly I was gripped by acute interest. The author, the Austrian philosopher, educator, and spiritual teacher Rudolf Steiner, was addressing the exact issue that had been turning over and over in my mind for the last year: the relationship between inner, subjective experience and the outer world perceptible to the senses.

I was gripped. This writer had both brilliance of intellect and a deep spiritual worldview, but also more than that. He had an intuitive understanding of the actual value of *feeling* for the human experience. As someone who had been educated in the dry rationalism of the British university system, and who had always experienced a strong, sometimes uncontrollable emotional life, it was an immense relief to encounter a deep philosophical mind that viewed the realm of "feeling" as equally essential to the full human experience as "thinking" and "willing." Every time I came across the use of the term "feeling," I wanted to shout an affirmation of joy. Here, at last, was a philosopher who made me feel whole.

I dived into the book and read it in a blaze of total absorption from cover to cover. Since my time in the Southwestern deserts in 1970, I had known mystical experiences, and had read widely from the sacred literature of many diverse traditions — Native American, Indian, Taoist, Tibetan Buddhist, shamanic, and psychedelic. But this felt like coming home. Ever since Banyen Books, that tiny hole in the wall in Kitsilano, Vancouver that was a spiritual oasis at a difficult time of searching and worrying, I had known of Rudolf Steiner. I had sat among the stacks of books, the saints and yogis gazing down from the shelves, reading, reading, reading, trying to find words that expressed an understanding of the kind of mystical experience that had led me to leave graduate school and set off in search of deeper truths than those then available in academia.

Rudolf Steiner's work had seemed impressive, but each time I opened a book, I came across language that meant little to me: etheric and astral bodies, cultural epochs, the use of the term "ego" in a way I did not understand, references to hierarchies of angels that seemed like something out of Byzantine Christianity. But now, in the unlikely spot of a beach on Kaua'i, on the opposite side of the planet from Steiner's native Austria, it all began to fall into place.

Here was a true lover of wisdom, a genuine philosopher engaged with the great enigmas and mysteries of the human condition. His worldview can be described as exquisite, beautiful, moving. For the next few years, my idea of a good weekend was to spend it absorbed in Steiner's seemingly endless works. His 6,000 different lectures had been collected into about 350 volumes, and he'd written over twenty books during a life that started in a small country village on the borders of Croatia and Hungary, passed through the universities and coffeehouses of Vienna, and reached the Goethe and Schiller Archives in Weimar in the 1890s. Steiner had begun to speak at the beginning of the twentieth century on profound esoteric matters, and built from scratch a unique center for contemporary mysteries, known as the Goetheanum, perched on a hill outside Basel, Switzerland.

For Steiner, our teachers were simply our spiritual friends. And that's what he has been to me — a wise, immensely knowledgeable, loving, and brilliant friend to whom I can reliably turn for insight into the most profound questions. I will never be the kind to follow a guru. I'm too much of an independent and free spirit. But I am happy to acknowledge genius when I see it. There have been few people in this world with Rudolf Steiner's intellectual breadth, spiritual depth, and total integrity. When we read the many insightful people who knew him personally, from the Russian novelist Andrei Bely to the German writer Christian Morgenstern to the Austrian master of the novella Stefan Zweig to the humanitarian Albert Schweitzer, they are in accord in regard to his warmth, his extraordinary insight, and the far-reaching quality of his mind.

Steiner viewed himself as an "initiate" — one initiated into the deepest mysteries of the cosmos. In Ancient Greece, it was the role of the initiates trained in such mystery centers as Delphi and Eleusis to guide the community in its relationship with the earth and the cosmos, in the celebration of seasonal festivals, and in the building of sacred places.

But entry into the mysteries had been confined to the carefully chosen few. In the modern age, the formerly secret holy wisdom was accessible to anyone who inquired. This form of holy wisdom, like Steiner himself, was intellectually acute, politically savvy, deeply conscious of the need to understand the nature of evil and the means to overcome it. And it was filled with beautiful meditative exercises.

In short, he was a brilliant guide on the road to an authentic spirituality. As with Jung, this work reconciled my spiritual and intellectual selves. It rooted me in the Western intellectual tradition in a way that left me open to, and appreciative of, all other paths. When I am in the Islamic world I feel that I'm a Sufi; when in the Celtic world a nature mystic; and when I enter the jungle and the great wilderness, I feel that I am on the path of the shaman. But thanks to Steiner, I feel grounded in a vast understanding of a cosmos that is spiritually alive, layered with endless mysteries, and supportive of my own evolution to ever-more whole levels of understanding and wisdom.

Rudolf Steiner knew fulfillment and sorrow, achievement and loss, deep loneliness and the joy of community, the happiness of thousands awakening to the value and truth of his work, and the heartbreak of a world tumbling into the abyss of World War I. In the course of my life I have been exposed to innumerable spiritual traditions from outside the usual Western canon, and have listened to, and learned from, depth psychologists who helped me to deal with the worries and questions of youth. But the main teacher to remain with me over the last thirty years is the sober, highly focused, and inestimably deep Rudolf Steiner.

A man capable of both tightly reasoned philosophical thinking and penetrating spiritual vision, he remains a unique figure in the landscape of twentieth-century spirituality, one that is awaiting discovery by the vast majority of "spiritual seekers" today.

Most of those who know about his legacy think of the Waldorf Schools, now the largest independent approach to education in the world, or the biodynamic farms that have led the way in the rediscovery of organic farming and now provide some of the finest wines, teas, and coffees. Or perhaps some think of the Camphill

Communities for special-needs children and adults that are present on every continent.

Steiner has left the most impressive holistic legacy of our time and a treasure chest of sacred wisdom. And yet he remains largely unread in holistic circles, at least in America. He was never one for pop spirituality. In the tradition of Central European philosophers, he engaged with the big picture, which for him meant the destiny of humanity, the fate of the Earth, and the evolution of consciousness.

Steiner's work includes a detailed description of a subtle human anatomy that can be perplexing for those first encountering it. He speaks of angelic worlds, of multiple incarnations and the operations of karma. Throughout it all his words are permeated with love and a great regard for human freedom.

Among the many who knew him, no one ever reported anything disturbing or scandalous. He was, in fact, a person of the highest integrity who appears to have done exactly what he said he would do — pass on to humanity a renewed spiritual worldview compatible with contemporary life.

I encountered his wisdom at a time in my life when I was looking to deepen my esoteric understanding. I count it a blessing, in fact, that I did not really respond to Steiner until I was in my mid-thirties and had already explored multiple spiritual paths. As a result of this, I was never tempted to immerse myself exclusively in anthroposophy, the title he gave to the path he opened to higher worlds and that points toward the deepest holy wisdom latent in humanity, awaiting self-realization. It is my belief that if he were alive today he would be delighted by the renewal of so many half-forgotten spiritual traditions and would wish for anthroposophists to reach out to other wisdom streams and celebrate their elements of commonality with his own teachings.

Rudolf Steiner took the view that human experience is fundamentally unintelligible and filled with countless insoluble riddles and enigmas. He felt that one ought to investigate esoteric wisdom with every fiber of honesty, intelligence, and strength that one could muster. I can only agree. Since childhood I have wanted to know why we are here, what the purpose of human life is, and how we can lead a life of meaning. In Steiner's work I found a non-dogmatic lover of wisdom who saw his task as engaging with these core questions. In fact, he considered doing so his profound responsibility as a contemporary philosopher. May there be many more like him in the centuries ahead!

∞

CHAPTER THIRTEEN

REDISCOVERING THE
LOST SPIRITUAL HISTORY
OF THE WEST

IN PRAISE OF BOHEMIA

I have always been a bohemian at heart, but little did I know that the country itself, or the Czech Republic as it is now called, would open a door to the deep stream of wisdom known as the Western Esoteric Tradition that would become a spiritual focal point of my life and bring countless blessings.

As the name suggests, Bohemia is the country most evocative of the Renaissance world of alchemists, kabbalists, and hermetic philosophers, and an aura of magic and beauty still hangs over Prague.

It was late one night in the early '90s, in southern Bohemia's mecca of alchemists, that I stumbled into a distant world, and a door opened into my work on the renewal of Western Esoteric Tradition.

After a Centers' Gathering in Bavaria, at a farm an hour east of Munich, I was traveling with a friend, Brigitte, from ZIST (the Center for Individual and Social Therapy, a kind of Esalen in the Bavarian Alps), entering a sleepy town nestled deep in the forests of the Šumava Mountains. This region had been hidden behind the Iron Curtain for half a century, and few Westerners knew much about it. We passed beneath a stone archway, and drove slowly along the dimly lit and deserted cobbled streets. We turned a corner and crossed a wide wooden bridge. Suddenly a high castle rose up from the river's edge. To its right was a tower perfectly illuminated that exuded a sense of harmony and proportion. This small town had one of the strongest auras of mystery I'd ever encountered. It felt like we had passed through some kind of time warp and were entering the sixteenth century.

In the morning, when I threw open the casement windows of the Renaissance seminary where we had spent the night, the room was filled with birdsong and the rushing of the Vltava River below. In the breakfast room I noticed that the walls displayed large red roses on every side. It slowly began to dawn on me that we had entered the world of the Rosicrucian Enlightenment as described by the great historian Frances Yates. Almost singlehandedly, she had re-created a lost epoch in the cultural history of Europe during the sixteenth and seventeenth centuries when the spiritual influence of Ficino and Pico's Florence had spread north, mixed with alchemy, and found favor with the Holy Roman Emperor himself, Rudolf II, and with a circle of Bohemian aristocrats, prominent among whom was Rožmberk, lord of the castle of Český Krumlov.

Between 1570 and 1620, the practitioners of the esoteric arts, spiritual explorers in the last age before the rise of the scientific worldview, had sought wisdom and enlightenment through a focused meditative experience of crystallization, combustion, and dissolution — salt, sulfur, and mercury in the symbolic language and imagery of the time. For every serious alchemist, there was both an inner and outer aspect of the work. As the Powder Tower of the Belvedere in Prague shows so clearly, below was the "laboratorio," where physical alchemy took place; above was the "oratorio" for the practice of spiritual alchemy. *As above, so below,* in the pithy words of the Emerald Tablet of Hermes Trismegistus.

This period had cast its charm over me thanks to the scholarship and storytelling of the redoubtable Dame Frances. Now I saw an opportunity to bring it alive again in the twentieth century. Could I bring an international audience to Český Krumlov to enter imaginatively the history and mystery of the alchemical world of Renaissance Bohemia?

It took three years to do it, but when, eventually, I invited every writer and scholar on the Western Tradition that I admired, I was stunned to receive acceptances from all of them. In this mostly unknown corner of Central Europe, there took place an "Esoteric Woodstock," in the words of *Gnosis* magazine, with Joscelyn Godwin, Christopher Bamford, Nicholas Goodrick-Clarke, Christopher McIntosh, and many deeply knowledgeable speakers on "the more powerful philosophy," as it was known in the sixteenth century. Little did I know that this seminal event would launch a twenty-year (and counting) series of conferences and Quests intended to aid in the rediscovery of the half-forgotten spiritual history of the West.

But I did know there was genuine magic in our gathering. As I walked the cobbled streets of Český Krumlov on my way to a candlelit poetry reading by Robert Bly in the Renaissance room of the alchemical castle, the full moon rose serenely from behind the hermetic tower. Who had choreographed this? It certainly wasn't me. Of course, the Quest had taken me into heightened states of consciousness in which synchronicities arose with grace and frequency. But there could be little doubt that something seminal had taken place in this archetypally faraway place. And that a new dimension of my life and work was opening.

Sadly, this extraordinary period in the esoteric history of Europe came to a shocking and premature end at the Battle of the White Mountain on a hilltop outside Prague in 1620, and Europe tumbled into the nightmare of the Thirty Years' War. When it finally emerged from the chaos, the worldview of scientific materialism — with its understanding of the mind as fully separate from the body, and the cosmos as a giant machine — was dawning. The wisdom and beauty contained in the alchemical, hermetic, and kabbalistic modes of thought and spiritual research were marginalized, and the West began its long march toward industrialization, the exploitation of natural resources, and ultimately worldwide environmental crisis.

The alchemists considered themselves "philosophers of nature"; they possessed an ecological sense of participation in a living universe filled with spiritual secrets waiting to be revealed. Fortunately, this more holistic approach to science was not to disappear forever. It reemerged in the late eighteenth century in Goethe's worldview employing a fresh form suited for the modern age, and found brilliant expression in Rudolf Steiner's enormous gift to the modern world — whose brilliance we are only beginning to understand.

★ ★ ★ ★ ★

The rediscovery of this half-forgotten realm has become, somewhat to my surprise, an enduring way to make a contribution of value. Perhaps in a future book, I will take readers more deeply into many mysterious and profound worlds. This journey of reclamation offers countless glimpses of holy wisdom in its ancient, medieval, renaissance, and more contemporary forms. Delight and wonder meet the eye at every turn.

The "Esoteric Quest," the series of conferences and journeys that I have now been privileged to direct for more than twenty years, has brought its participants a taste of the ancient mystery centers that encircled the Aegean Sea, a chance to feel in their heart's core the brilliant cosmopolitan culture of Greco-Egyptian Alexandria, and a doorway into the golden age of Andalusia, with its Sufis, kabbalists, and philosophers. We have contemplated the beauty of the soul of the Renaissance while watching the full moon rise and the golden sun set behind the Tuscan hills in perfect cosmic harmony. In search of the esoteric wisdom of Central Europe we traveled from the alchemical world of Renaissance Bohemia through the liminal realm of Marienbad to Goethe's Weimar.

This Quest for truth and wisdom, taken in the company of others, has brought alive in my imagination many distant worlds, from sixteenth-century Bohemia to the mysteries of Aphrodite in Cyprus to the ancient Greek civilization of Sicily. I even have been privileged to glimpse and taste the ecstasies practiced by Sufi brotherhoods in the medina of Marrakesh, the Asian shore of Istanbul, and the backstreets of Alexandria. Much remains to be told of these realms and epochs — at another time and in another place.

The Quest has also given me a way to see my own life from a fresh and helpful perspective. The philosophies of antiquity revived in the Renaissance reveal a worldview in which humanity is deeply connected to the cosmos. The philosopher and the natural magician in fifteenth-century Florence or sixteenth-century Bohemia aimed to live and work in sympathetic resonance with the movements of the planets, the alignments of the stars, the seasons of the year, the temperaments of the human being.

Drawing on this perspective, and on archetypal psychology, I came to ponder my life after thirty years in New York. Perhaps it was time to find a new balance. After decades of the Saturnine weight of responsibility on my shoulders, multiple deadlines and Mercurial phone calls, a constant stream of messages to return and catalogues to produce, it was time to enter a new phase. From this perspective, I could see that I needed to enjoy more of the harmonizing influences of Jupiter, Venus, and Sol — that Jovial ease and relaxation, the Venusian presence of beauty and art, and the Sun's luminous, musical influence to chase away the dark shadows of big-city life. It was time for change.

And so, I contemplate the future. If life is a three-act play, I am now entering the third act, one of unknown duration. My task now is to find a balance between the inner and outer realms of existence, between spiritual contemplation and societal engagement, between pursuing wisdom and practicing love, and between the multiple ideas and ways of being coming to us all now from the West, East, North, and South so that a free, tolerant, and multicultural world can evolve further in this century for the benefit of all.

And so I conclude on a note of gratitude. Without my stumbles, doubts, and dark times, or my joys, ecstasies, and insights, I would never have uncovered the trail that leads toward the Jeweled Highway. But, once found, that road goes on forever.

EPILOGUE

This book has been an account of one personal experience in the midst of a subtle but pervasive cultural change. I have tried to recall what it felt like to set out on my quest for a deeper view of reality; my questions and adventures; my involvement in strong initiatives to bring about a saner and more sustainable world; and my discovery of the beauty of the Western spiritual and philosophical tradition after a sustained immersion in other cultures and spiritual practices.

Although I have traveled extensively, my daily life has been intimately involved in producing and directing many hundreds of events, mostly in New York City, all of which have been intended to support and develop a more holistic, organic, and sustainable way of being in the world. Over 300,000 participants have attended programs at the Open Center since its inception; and, whatever the future holds, this is a track record in which I feel my colleagues and I can find satisfaction. When I think of the countless lives that have, in some way, benefited from these experiences, my heart is glad.

I have not gone into detail about the many outstanding speakers and teachers with whom I have had the pleasure of working. Suffice it to say that it has been a deep privilege to work with so many gifted, wise, creative, and awake people and draw on their dedication, knowledge, and wisdom. Without them, the Open Center could have achieved nothing.

Nor have I attempted to cover in detail the many themes the Center and its worldwide friends and colleagues have addressed — including integrative health, inner development, world spiritual traditions, the arts, and environmental and social change — that have formed the backbone of our work. Others have covered these themes in comprehensive ways.

The creation of this center of holistic learning has not taken place in a vacuum. While poverty and income inequality remain enduring problems, New York City itself has undergone an enormous transformation for the better in the last thirty years. The relentless crime and violence that permeated the city when the Open Center began are an increasingly distant memory. Instead the city has embraced the goal of becoming a leading eco-city in the twenty-first century, and is planting a million new trees and fostering green initiatives from urban farms to hybrid buses. No one would have imagined this emergence of an incipient eco-metropolis from the chaos of a city synonymous with mayhem and danger just a few years ago. Even Queens, my main home for the last twenty years, has begun to shift in public perception from a neglected, somewhat embarrassing outer borough devoid of cool or charm to recognition as the world's most multicultural destination, where more languages are spoken than anywhere else on earth. Certainly anyone who tries to dismiss our emerging multicultural future as impractical should take a ride on the Number 7 subway through Queens and see how well people from literally all over the world coexist, and even find pleasure in their differences.

As the world struggles between competing visions of the future, and the dark powers of religious fundamentalism, retrograde nationalism, and relentless, shortsighted materialism seek to influence future generations, we cannot create a healthy future without addressing core questions of meaning and purpose. The fact is that the hollow consumerism of the West is an insufficiently compelling narrative to grip the psyches of young people and inspire them to devote themselves to a more just and harmonious future. Holistic centers and writers, the emerging worldwide network of ecovillages, plus countless festivals such as Burning Man in the Nevada desert allow the invigorated soul of the world to emerge in freedom, and for values and modes of living together to develop that offer serious alternatives to our overworked, under-slept, often depressed societies. The holistic worldview in all its countless variations offers true hope and inspiration for the future, leads us away from destructive climate change, and contains plenty of room for excitement, innovation, and adventure.

I hope my story makes clear that not everyone who went through the late '60s and early '70s, with its cocktail of taboo-breaking and uncensored exploration, disappeared into addiction or hopelessness. Many of us experienced an enduring opening of consciousness that has enabled us to devote our lives to the creation of a more positive future.

How has it felt to do this for decades? At times it has been wearying, discouraging, a heavy burden. At other times, and they are in the majority, it has felt inspiring, a gift, and a joy. I have had the good fortune to receive a unique education from the myriad speakers and teachers who I invited to teach. And there is immense satisfaction in this work, a true nourishment of the soul.

The holistic impulse is only one of many creative forces working for positive change today. It is accompanied by the transcendence of racism, prejudice, and numerous forms of political, economic, and environmental exploitation. I admire those whose path has more directly involved political engagement with these great issues and the courage required to face the ugliness, brutality, and invasion of privacy that often entails. As a politically attuned person, I have at times sought to bring holistic perspectives into the political arena by efforts to reimagine our society through a fresh political and economic lens. But my main work has been as a cultural activist, an evolutionary perhaps rather than a revolutionary, a propagator of change through education, experience, and awakening, not through force or the ballot box.

As I look back, I see a quiet boy in austerity Cardiff, living in the terraced streets, playing among the bombsites as a four-year-old. Then a little older on the shores of the Irish Sea, the row houses replaced by the limestone headland of the Little Orme, thrilling to the endless sound of crying seagulls, loving the steady rhythm of the gray sea, gazing on the Snowdonian peaks. I recall the alienated teenager in a grimy, industrial town in Northern England, feeling trapped and depressed, saved only by rock and roll as a beam of light in a dark landscape. Then it was on to the academic equivalent of Swinging London, a taste of freedom and ecstasy at last.

My inner life began in earnest on a road trip down Route 66 with its spiritual awakening among the beauty of the Southwestern deserts and mountains. From there as a young adult my path led to a sustained taste of the counterculture, sometimes confused and worried, many times lonely and broke, often not knowing where my life would take me or where my income would come from. Those difficult times were very real but they were an inescapable part of finding a meaningful life. I'd like readers to come away from this book knowing that even with those arduous moments, the journey has been well worth it. I feel fortunate to have lived a life rich in experience, meeting and learning from some of the most aware and clear-sighted people of our era, and creating opportunities for others to have similar experiences.

I end this book feeling fortunate that so many trails and avenues have opened into the great mystery at the heart of existence. I have also been fortunate in having a deeply loving partner, Nanette, whose sustained support has been of inestimable value now for many years. The journey has had no shortage of detours, and there have been times when the trail appeared to grow faint and thin. But life has only strengthened my conviction that an inner radiance lies at the heart of each human being awaiting discovery and expression, and that our vast cosmos ultimately supports those who set out to find it. I hope this story of my own path brings some inspiration and encouragement to others. Through it all, I have tried to use as my guide the fount of love implanted in my heart, to walk the path of honest thought, and to read as best I can the cosmic script spread out before us all.

ABOUT THE AUTHOR

Photo: Ralph White

RALPH WHITE is cofounder of the New York Open Center (*www.opencenter.org*), the city's leading venue for holistic learning since 1984, where for many years he has served as director, program director, and senior fellow. A writer, lecturer, radio host, organizer, creative director, editor, and world traveler, he is a pioneer in the global-consciousness movement, and has created and produced many hundreds of conferences, workshops, and performances across the spectrum of holistic learning. His current activities include the Esoteric Quest series of conferences in Europe on the lost spiritual history of the West (*www.esotericquest.org*) that have continued for twenty years, and the Art of Dying conferences (*www.artofdying.org*) that address the emergence of a more holistic understanding of death in contemporary America. From 1995 to 2001 he edited *Lapis* magazine, winner of the Alternative Press Award 2000 from *Utne Reader*. He has also taught at New York University and has been a seminal presence in the development of the global network of holistic centers. (*www.centersgathering.org*)

Born in Wales, he lives in New York City. (*www.ralphwhite.net*)

ALSO FROM DIVINE ARTS

THE SHAMAN & AYAHUASCA: *Journeys to Sacred Realms*
Don José Campos   2013 Nautilus Silver Medalist

"This remarkable book suggests a path back to understanding the profound healing and spiritual powers that are here for us in the plant world, reawakening our respect for the natural world, and thus for ourselves."
—John Robbins, author of *Diet for a New America*

ONWARD & UPWARD: *Reflections of a Joyful Life*
Michael Wiese   2014 COVR Award Winner

"Onward & Upward is the memoir of a rare and wonderful man who has lived a truly extraordinary life. It's filled with Michael Wiese's adventures, his incredible journeys, and his interactions with amazing people."
—John Robbins, author of *Diet for a New America*

RECIPES FOR A SACRED LIFE:
True Stories and a Few Miracles
Rivvy Neshama   2013 IPPY Gold Award Winner

"Neshama's stories are uplifting, witty, and wise: one can't go wrong with a recipe like that. The timeless wisdom she serves up is food for the soul."
—*Publishers Weekly*

SOPHIA—THE FEMININE FACE OF GOD:
Nine Heart Paths to Healing and Abundance
Karen Speerstra   2013 Nautilus Silver Medalist

"Karen Speerstra shows us most compellingly that when we open our hearts, we discover the wisdom of the Feminie all around us. A totally refreshing exploration and beautifully researched read."
—Michael Cecil, author of *Living at the Heart of Creation*

THE JEWELED HIGHWAY: *On the Quest for a Life of Meaning*
Ralph White

"Ralph White's luminous memoirs embrace the spiritual sphere of multiple revelations and portray a love of Gaia, our planet, as perhaps no one has done before. If some modern revelation has appeared on our planet, Ralph has been there, not in control, but willing to participate and be affected. The Jeweled Highway is vital and alive and not constrained by ideology or political correctness. It is Dionysian, a voyage without a plan, a trust in serendipity, an appreciation of love over logic."
—Thomas Moore, author of *Care of the Soul*

THE DIVINE ART OF DYING: *How to Live Well While Dying*
Karen Speerstra & Herbert Anderson, Foreword by Ira Byock, MD

"A magnificent achievement. The Divine Art of Dying is a moving and inspiring book about taking control of your life as it starts to come to a close."
— Will Schwalbe, author of the *New York Times*–bestselling *The End of Your Life Book Club*

LIVING BEYOND THE FIVE SENSES:
The Emergence of a Spiritual Being
Teresa L. DeCicco, PhD

"Teresa DeCicco articulates clearly and eloquently the age-old exploration of transformation, spirituality, and religion from an insider's perspective: as a woman who's experienced the richness of life beyond the five senses."
—Lisa Wimberger, author of *New Beliefs, New Brain*

FREE YOUR MIND: *A Meditation Guide to Freedom and Happiness*
Ajay Kapoor

"Free Your Mind goes beyond today's fashionable mindfulness movement by using our thinking, rather than simply noting it. Kapoor carefully shows us how to use our minds to break down our mental conditioning and become truly free."
— Franz Metcalf, author of *What Would Buddha Do?*

LIVING IN BALANCE: *A Mindful Guide for Thriving in a Complex World*
Joel & Michelle Levey, Foreword by His Holiness the Dalai Lama

"Joel and Michelle have constructed a text of sheer brilliance. Every page offers new insights and truth."
—Caroline M. Myss, PhD, author of *Why People Don't Heal and How They Can* and *Anatomy of the Spirit*

THE POWER OF I AM: *Aligning the Chakras of Consciousness*
Geoffrey Jowett

"Geof Jowett is a healer, mystic, and altogether a wonderful spiritual teacher. Science and Spirit mix beautifully with him."
—James Van Praagh, author of the # 1 *New York Times* bestseller *Talking to Heaven*

Celebrating the sacred in everyday life.

Divine Arts was founded to share some of the new and ancient knowledge that is rapidly emerging from the scientific, indigenous, and wisdom cultures of the world, and to present new voices that express eternal truths in innovative, accessible ways.

Although the Earth appears to be in a dark state of affairs, we have realized from the shifts in our own consciousness that millions of beings are seeking and finding a new and optimistic understanding of the nature of reality; and we are committed to sharing their evolving insights.

Our esteemed authors, masters and teachers from around the world, have come together from all spiritual practices to create Divine Arts books. Our unity comes in celebrating the sacredness of life and in having the intention that our work will assist in raising human consciousness and benefiting all sentient beings.

We trust that our work will serve you,
and we welcome your feedback.

Michael Wiese, *Publisher*

DIVINE ARTS | DIVINEARTSMEDIA.COM